FEAR (LESS) FRIDAYS

Notes from a small woman living in a Big Big world

Vikki Spencer, M.Ed.

This book is a reluctant memoir. It reflects the author's present recollections of experiences over time, which only get more epic as time goes on, so I'm writing them now. Some names and characteristics have been changed, some have not. Some people have been left out. It happens. All events have been compressed because it's long enough. All dialogue has been recreated and chosen for the juicy bits. According to me.

Paperback ISBN-13: 978-0-578-43544-2

First Edition

Cover art design by: Evocative at 99Designs.com

Author Photo by: Bekah Morton Photography

Dedicated To:

My 673 Facebook friends who liked, loved, and walked with me every Friday these past few years. Your showing up kept me showing up.

This is for all of us who are trying to be a little less afraid, and for the people who love us through it.

Contents

Preface

Fear(Less) Fridays became my answer to proving my online friend, and yoga instructor, Kolleen Harrison, completely wrong.

Sometime in 2016, she asked in a Facebook post, "What stops you from moving forward?" I answered, "I'm chicken of everything. Afraid of everything that might be."

She replied, "F. fear. It's a liar. It's holding back your brilliance from us...". Fear lying? Brilliance? How sad for someone to stay locked up because of perceptions. How sad for them. But coming from the shadows of fear felt viscerally threatening. *I'll show you, Kolleen, how wrong you are. I have NO brilliance. NO one will even care.* Except, hiding held me captive in a world of no decisions, movement, success or failure. So, the challenge was now, *What if I do borrow your perspective and just show up anyway? Once a week.*

I can't be fearless. Maybe some can be, but I can't.

But I can fear less: find my fear, listen to it, and notch it down just a bit. Then what would I find? I didn't know. I'd have to face what freaks me out. I have been afraid of being in natural disasters, loss, divorce, death, friends leaving, messing up my business, burglaries, being alone, losing my home, accepting toxic people, and wasting money and/or time, of being seen in any way, shape or form, of doing life wrong and of being too much or not enough.

I've been afraid of having drugs planted on me, being mistaken for someone else, causing a car accident, being in a car accident, inadvertently ending up in a sex trafficking ring or messing up my kid and taking responsibility for any failure he brought on himself. Before noon today.

Other than that, I was good. ;-)

So, I started posting on Facebook under #FearLessFriday, a weekly lifeline to show up and find my edges and face fears of being seen. My only guide was to answer the questions, "What do you NOT want to share today? What is true for you?" This meant no posts where I needed affirmation or therapy. I was literally just sharing past experiences—that was scary enough when you're trying to hide and stay safe. Even still, I cried because it was hard, and embarrassing and wimpy. THEN I cried because people didn't troll me or ignore me but walked with me in encouragement and love, and I didn't feel I deserved it at all.

I'm including posts that are not technically "FearLess Fridays." They are very much in the spirit of them but are included for background and context: that I thought I had more of my life together than I actually did. Some are a foreboding inspiration of what I would need later…the early rumblings of what life had in store.

The original Friday post and a few after that, where I was pretty sure I'd prove Kolleen wrong, was about my business, The Mom Whisperer. But it quickly changes and progresses, and gets more personal, as you'll see. I'd rather delete these; however, I'm keeping them because progression and growth seem an antidote to fear. Maybe seeing how everything is a process, matters.

Little did any of us realize it would be the singularly worst years of my life with nearly 13 life losses in two and a half years. And I would keep writing anyway. It was an act of life and showing up when everything familiar disappeared one by one, like Jenga blocks being poked away from unexpected places.

What started as How to Show Up to Life Even When You're Afraid within months became, How to Show Up to Life When It's Falling Apart, and You're Really Afraid. Is it best to just hole up and not live? Really? What happens if we keep moving forward, however, we can, through fear — not around it? Do all our worst fears come true? Heh. Sometimes.

There was also a series of 10 weeks where I went MIA from all screens and social media. I've never talked about those missing weeks. This silence wasn't because of fear, but to honor myself and whatever process was needed to cocoon and heal. I'm choosing to share it because very often people say I project "confidence, strength and courage." Yet, at my core, I'm *always* anxious, afraid, and doubting myself relentlessly. Since I'm almost two years away from this time, now I'd like to show honestly what happened with grief, healing, and re-learning how to live.

After the 10 weeks, the posts carry a different weight, measure, and love. They feel less sure but more open—hearted.

A little heads up on what you're embarking on. On the advice of a friend, I've taken off the dates of the posts, although they happened in order. There are quote pages that were posted earlier, and I mix those in to give us space and air from the intensity of the stories. With the permission of friends, many have allowed me to keep their names as is. I want to acknowledge the truth of the stories, and their courage to not hide either, and be eternally linked to me, in some of the best ways possible. I'm so glad you'll get to meet some of my friends in this way. They are a few of many who were wind to me.

The anecdotes are only half of what you think they are. My friends as the audience, with their perspective, support, laughter with me, and love, are actually the magic behind the posts that I can't convey in book form. Knowing I wasn't alone kept me going and sharing with perspectives that apparently helped others through their own private lives.

They asked me to compile them in one place. Sometimes it's because they wanted to encourage someone else. Sometimes it's because they wanted to remember what I wrote and didn't want to look through the three years I'd been writing. Every time they asked, I resisted the urge to hide in a bowl of frozen custard.

Hey, it's a process.

But here we are.

Please know this is not a novel, and again, happened over a large span of time. It's best enjoyed in spoonfuls. Every entry is a world in itself. Think bathroom book, not Sunday coffee shop binge. Listen, I still can't get through it all very quickly and I know the ending.

I am clearly not, nor will I ever be, the poster child for Fearlessness.

What I do hope is that as I commit to moving through fear, showing up anyway and doing the next thing, there's connection, hope and a few sticky notes of truth you can feel to toss back at me when I'm sideways and forget what I said.

So, come on in on our little weekly secret and find good company.

Because facing fear is always where we start.

But where we end up is often more beautiful than we ever imagined. Truly, I've been learning that everything I've ever wanted is on the other side of fearing just a little bit less.

Grateful you're here, *Vikki*

CHAPTER #1

Game On

Just for the record, I'm a wuss. A wimp. The only thing brave about me is that I can surf. This year I'm trying to get over it.

I'm trying to stop hearing a friend say, "Just do one thing every day that scares the crap out of you." But I can't. She's right, even if I don't know how to actually pull that off.

I'm not playing small this year. Ok. I am. But I'm going to try to make other choices.

"Everything tells me that I am about to make a wrong decision, but making mistakes is just part of life. What does the world want of me? Does it want me to take no risks, to go back to where I came from because I didn't have the courage to say "yes" to life?"

— Paulo Coelho, Eleven Minutes

Posted in January 2013. On the day I agreed to living one more year as an unhappily married woman, trying to make my entire life work just the way I wanted it to. Apparently, this was my stake in the ground reverberating through my entire life.

CHAPTER #2

On Being Right

You may be 100% right about another person.
But you still have no power to change them.
— My journal notes from a second visit to The National Institute of Marriage

CHAPTER #3

On Grandma's Birthday

Today is my Gram's 95th birthday. She said, "I'm surprised I made it!"

Every year the whole family lives as if it's her last — leaning in, celebrating. For us, that means spending tons of time together, eating dinner at 4:30pm, washing dishes and drying them together, and playing Scrabble while Gram beats us every.single.time. We've spent 15 years absolutely with no regrets, and loving without fear of loss. Maybe it feels like a false alarm every year. Or it's so matter—of—fact, we're a bit immune to the goodbye.

Easy to say when we're healthy, and not saying goodbye yet.

But now, she has cancer.

We've all talked about her death with her, and she's as coherent and clear about accepting an end.

I think it's because she's suffering and won't tell us how much. Or how she's missing Gramp and looking forward to seeing him again.

She always says she's ready any time now.

I told her to wait until after she visits us and goes to the craft fair in November. She said, "Sounds good!"

But maybe that's too long. And maybe Gramp misses her too.

Maybe she doesn't really care about the craft fair after all.

And maybe the flight is too long, thc airport too large to get through for someone who consistently refuses a wheelchair, at 95, with cancer.

If I say, "Don't come," she'll say she has nothing to look forward to.

So, it's either our family or Gramp.

And either way, she wins.

CHAPTER #4

The Deal of a Lifetime

Today I don't care about the free stuff, good deals, best ways to... or any other way to make my life better, faster, more productive or perfect other than to live it.

CHAPTER #5

Waiting On God for 7 Days

A friend said over lunch they felt I was running ahead of God on something.

I've heard it a million times.

Apparently, I am too fast for God. I need more patience. I'm not giving God time. I'm not patient enough. I'm supposed to wait… on what I'm never sure.

I'm supposed to be a good girl and wait.

After two days I realized: I would rather have the theology of a God who goes before me even if just to turn me around rather than believe in a God who somehow can't handle me moving forward.

On Day 3, I wondered if men get told they are running ahead of God as much as women do.

On Day 4, I suspected God was already ahead of me cheering me on.

On Day 5, I felt God before me, beside me, behind me, and above me.

On Day 6, I realized God within me.

And on day 7, I took a nap. ;-)

CHAPTER #6

The Actual Perk of Happiness

About two and a half years ago, I sat with a book called, *The How of Happiness* by Sonja Lyubomirsky with a few squares of dark chocolate in hand.

Between that, prayer, great friends, pursuit of dreams and laughing, I can say that right now bliss is chasing me. Bliss, ya'll. Not EVEN just happiness.

Ok naysayers, I could list 10 things daily to complain about, but they are situations not necessarily under my control.

Choosing happiness, or at least a positive, grateful perspective and keeping a smile on my face in the midst of unexpected conversations or conflict makes others a little on edge...or calms them down.

Their choice.

Mine is another round of dark chocolate, and a few, long overdue thank-you notes.

CHAPTER #7

When It All Falls Apart

My 16-year-old son, Jordan, and I were in a tornado—type storm that flung three trees on the house, and 15 more across the land we live on.

The roof is damaged, as is the chimney.

We are okay.

But in less than 24 hours here's what I'm learning about life after a storm:

Most will not understand the loss.

Some will say their loss was worse.

Many will ask if help is needed then disappear.

One or two will hug and or say, "I'm so sorry" and just look at it with you.

One will contact you and say they heard and can't get there but can't imagine... thinking of you.

Those last two are the keepers.

As in the physical world, so also in the spiritual and emotional worlds.

CHAPTER #8

It May Take Awhile

With the trees topping 150 feet tossed around the backyard like toothpicks, my stepmother, Leslie, suggested I visit local farms and ask if they need firewood.

Three farms later, no takers.

But word got out.

And one farmer knew another.

An old—timer in jean overalls and a baseball cap stopped by and asked me if I knew whom my neighbor was.

I told him about Farmer Joe.

"Have you had words with him?"

"No, sir."

Farmer Joe had the only street access to my property, meaning I'd need permission for logging trucks to cross his property to get to mine- if I could even find a logging company that would take the twisted wood away.

I didn't know him. Just rumors that he's tough and doesn't always like to be helpful.

Apparently, when you live in the old south, there's always a catch to trying to be a good neighbor. So, everyone is on guard wondering what the ulterior motives are. Farmer Joe came over with his friend and eyed the damage.

I was kind but said, "If your land wasn't clear cut this past summer, my trees would have been able to survive and not take a direct hit from the winds. I'm not blaming anyone, but I need help here."

Apparently, he owns a sawmill. And he would like to have the wood from the oak, birch, and poplars.

He asked how much I wanted for the load of wood.

I asked how much he wanted to remove it...and smiled.

I said I bet we could call it even.

He would also like to take it out himself if that's okay. He just needs time. He needs to harvest crops and bale hay.

So if I'll give him some time, he'll be back to clean it up.

So interesting.

What I see as a messed up backyard, and no less than $7000 expense that insurance won't cover, is his opportunity.

Truth is, most of the wood is so twisted, it may not be salvageable.

God sees and is often laughing at my face when I see how He provides.

Updated: God isn't laughing at my face. Ever.

At least now I know.

I wish I knew that then.

Actually, this event would protect me in ways I would only find out much later.

CHAPTER #9

No Small Life

"The first step in the courageous conversation is to stop having the one you're having now. The second step is cultivating a relationship with the unknown." *--David Whyte interview with Krista Tippet, The Conversational Nature of Reality, On Being (4/7/2016) https://onbeing.org/programs/david-whyte-the-conversational-nature-of-reality/*

Ok, fine. So, here's the truth about the tornado and the trees, and things I don't want to say but want to tell you.

The weather was getting warmer and yet the house was colder. There was this Saturday of chores and cooking and the TV was on. Everything looked like a day in the life of us. But it was 9pm and but I remember thinking the last thing anyone said was around dinner at 6pm. By the evening, I asked to talk with him. I had nothing planned out. I listened, and talked and at the end, in tears I just realized a searing truth that I spoke.

"You deserve more. Jordan deserves more. I deserve more. I can't make my life any smaller and still, no one is happy. And my health is turning, and I'll be in the hospital within months. Take it all." I tapped out.

So, it really was on me, which you may have heard. (*Seriously, don't you ever just wonder what happens in the moments when people split?*)

Sunday, he left for a hotel, which I understood and supported completely. We were both reeling and exhausted. Maybe we were worn for longer than we realized.

Monday around 4 pm, Jordan and I were home. and a tornado ripped through our property, tossing trees on the house, the deck, and in the neighbor's yard. The firefighters told us it was a disaster area.

I called him, "So... I know things aren't great right now between us, but um...we're okay but the house…um...don't be worried when you come home. "

We tried to work as a team. But within a week we realized he couldn't work in the house that was now intermittent contractors and constant interruptions. Within weeks we decided who would live where and he allowed me to stay in the house so I could make repairs that, little did we know, would take over four months to coordinate.

I thought for a long time God was punishing me for some grievous choice, thought, action that I committed and forgot about--why else would He allow my marriage to run aground, and the trees to be destroyed? I told Him to take them all. Take everything. I was done.

Leaving a marriage feels like taking a butter knife to your right arm; holding one last time everything you banked your existence on and deciding to remove it from your body.

It's not that it doesn't hurt. You do it because if you don't, parts of you will die because you know they already are numb. Other parts feel as if they already left. You know you're in survival in a place that should be home. I wish I could explain it another way... I really can't.

But this is why when women ask me if they should leave or stay, I always say, "You know the person you think you'll be when you leave? Work on being that person now, because wherever you go, there you are. And its' hell to leave." Most stay- for all their right reasons.

I chose to stay then I chose not to.

That's what happened according to me.

All during this time odd gifts keep coming without my control, or help, or even knowing what to ask... healing takes many forms.

I am letting friends go and can't chase others. Help comes exactly how and when I needed it. Real friends surface, family is rallying. Just last week, the farmer is cleaning up the remaining trees.

God wasn't/ isn't punishing me. He was keeping me here. I was the only one with enough time to handle insurance, coordinating roofers, tree cutters, a farmer and chimney repairers. Otherwise, there were grounds to ask me to leave, since I spoke the unspeakable.

Of all the things that are helping me heal, it's been nature/ Creation, and a slow simmer of changing my cells, washing away tears, rooting and grounding me in a different way of being in the world.

Nature is teaching me you don't get over things or sometimes even through things — you are changed by them.

You are carved.

Or dismantled.

But then there's this inherent choice to trust and at least show up or stay in the bed.

Some days I do both.

And either way, I am loved and have to prove nothing for God and life to find me.

And now you know.

I'm not bringing this up again, even for context — because as I move forward, now you'll understand that every serendipitous person, event, and opportunity for the miracle that it is...even when I have to let go again. Because from here on, it's even more letting go... and even more watching what unfolds. ;-)

With great honor for all our journeys, may we all move toward who and where we were always most meant to be.

CHAPTER #10

Be The Change Anyway

I should have already done this... here we go.

Dear God,

You know the person who took my favorite magnet and the first one I ever bought for a car?

Well, I'm forgiving them.

They don't know the chaos I'm in the middle of.

They don't know the things that are falling apart and that I'm trying to hold onto. I can't even hold onto my car magnet.

And maybe they do know that right now I can't possibly "Be the Change You Want to See In The World" like the magnet reminded me.

So it's theirs.

I ask that You forgive them as well.

I really wanted someone to steal it from them, but let's just end it here, okay?

Just help them to really Be the Change in their World, even if it didn't start out that way… Love, me

CHAPTER #11

Permission for The New Year

Just so we're all on the same page, it's not too late to change your resolutions, your word for the year, your weight loss goals, or your mind.

It's not too late to change the company you keep, the dreams you weave, or the job you have or don't have.

In fact, maybe the gift of this new year may be to finally recognize what needs to change and what needs to stay.

Not because it keeps us safe, but because it's just who we are and aren't anymore.

CHAPTER #12

A Woman's Worth

Last week I stumbled into a jewelry store alone. I'm not sure if I was trying to find a non-wedding ring, or just look around.

I'm not sure why the sales people thought to ask about looking at the high dollar bracelets, or why I even thought to agree except it felt like a museum and I always wondered about what was behind the glass.

I was honored to briefly wear a $27,000 gold and diamond cuff for a full 60 seconds.

Two things I want to never, ever forget:

1) It's breathtakingly stunning and heavy. Really heavy.
2) I thought of how many women I wished were with me to put it on their wrist and tell them, "You're worth more than that. So much more."

CHAPTER #13

The Greatest Generation

My grandmother went heavenward yesterday.

It was nine months after the craft fair she never made it to.

Every month, feeling it was her last. She often asked, "How much longer?"

She worked making canvases for Army cots for World War II and yet just a few weeks ago face-timed me.

I cannot honor her only as "beautiful" — she was far more than that. She was a quiet powerhouse of love, of acceptance and of forgiveness.

She modeled sacrifice and commitment to family as being a joy. She never spoke a negative word about anyone that I can remember. She kicked our butts in Scrabble until she was 90.

And we laughed.

A few months ago, I asked her what she would want us to remember. She said, "Always forgive, stay healthy, and to remember that the best things in life really are free."

She lived that.

Every time one of you post about losing a grandparent, I always feel like we lose the threads of that "greatest generation." And your stories of them rumble through my head and heart for a few days. We'll add her to the roster. Will be in CT soon.

CHAPTER #14

$16 and Some Bread

Dear Person Who Found and Did Not Return My Wallet:

Here's the deal:

All the cards are useless.

Keys— useless, because we'll park another car behind mine or in the garage and you can't steal it anyway.

However, if you'll look toward the middle, there IS a filled-up card for a totally free loaf of AMAZING bread AND a filled-up card for 20% off a new bra.

You can have the $16. I'm giving it to you.

Thank you for expediting my new single life with a new wallet, cards, etc. Maybe consider sharing that $16.

I'm guessing you're under 40 because, after that age, we clearly know what goes around comes around.

Wishing you grace and bread and a great fitting bra.

CHAPTER #15

52 Card Pick Up

No one gets all 52 cards in the deck. Even the luckiest, highest profile person doesn't get all 52 cards.

If you have a family, money may be tight.

If you have work you love, you may be looking for love.

If you have money, you don't always know who to trust to just love you.

We all find the Jokers at some point.

There's always a tiny missing piece. Most of us focus on that one and forget the 50 cards we do hold.

So, I'm thinking that real life is to fiercely play the ones you have with joy, gratitude, and wisdom, knowing that if the other hands around the table were tipped, no one would trade.

CHAPTER #16

Messing With My Own Mind

Three Gratitude Challenges That Have Messed with My Mind In All The Best Ways:

1) Think of the thing/ person you are most angry at — and find a reason or lesson to be grateful for.
2) Think of the thing/ person you don't have that you wish you did — and find a reason to be grateful for the absence.
3) Think of one thing/ person you cannot change even though you have tried until you gave up — and find a reason to be grateful for it/ them.

Because at some point, we've got to expand our idea of "blessing."

CHAPTER #17

The Lesson of Love and Fire

So, there's this night in November when Jordan is at his dad's and I recognize my house but not my home.

And through tears, I decided to make a fire. Wood, matches... but nothing. I try for two hours. I try every weekend for a month—nothing. There never ever was a solid fire in that space, and I was determined to make this happen.

I started asking people "How do you make a fire?" and everyone had their one thing that worked... especially my stepmother, Leslie, who answered every call I made to her on Saturday nights. Eventually, I realized this was and wasn't about the fire... and all about love and a little about life.

Here's what I learned:

Every fireplace is different. There are essential elements, but you keep trying to see what combination works.

Ashes from past fires are the foundation. It's the insulator once you get it going but the first thing you have to have. Don't clean it out— use it.

Fat sticks are essential. They are wood and sap fire starters that will burn long enough to get the kindling burning because fire takes time.

Once the kindling is going THEN, you put thin logs on. In stages. Otherwise, everything gets snuffed out, and you start from the beginning.

Logs have to cross each other at some point to create heat and stay lit. That meeting point can be very small, but it can't be parallel, it has to intersect.

The logs used to keep it going really matter. I learned how to check the BTU's by feeling the weight. Not every log is ready to burn and dang it the only way you know is by putting it in the fire.

If a log doesn't burn, you add fat sticks and other logs around it. It may never burn. But the other logs keep the fire going around it.

There has to be air. The space at the top of the chimney has to have so much circulation that it sucks the air up, keeping the fire burning. Because of the trees that fell on the house, the chimney plate was damaged. Once this was fixed, I could make a fire every single time. Air is everything.

When it's time to put the fire out slowly, all that's needed is to remove the logs from each other. And water to quench flames. And close the doors, so the air is cut off.

And all that's needed to make another is a match, a little time, air, and a few fat sticks.

This past snow day, I asked J. if I could teach him how to build one.

"I thought we couldn't make a fire."

"We couldn't. But now we can. I've been learning. I don't need all the other things I thought I did. "

"I thought we needed a ton of stuff to make a fire— you only have like three things."

"Its' all we need."

CHAPTER #18

Official Request

Dear God,

After a year of single—handedly removing a snakeskin, removing those three birds from the house, picking off a dead mouse from Christmas decorations, facing all manner of spiders and bugs, getting the four dead trees removed, finally solving the leak in the side of the house, helping a seizing dog...

I officially STILL REQUEST the retreat ranch for women.

I just need to add a small staff to that request.

Thank you in advance. Amen

CHAPTER #19

Superpower

One of my superpowers: diffusing conflict.

One of my tragic flaws: sometimes I just don't want to.

What I learned: sometimes I don't need to.

CHAPTER #20

Just Do The Next Thing

I'm learning to trust that life
asks me to take as many steps as I possibly can,
without knowing exactly where it's going,
then without fail,
opens up possibilities,
connections and vistas bigger
than I was thinking.
Even though I was thinking pretty big.
Just do the next thing.

CHAPTER #21

That Time I Didn't Hate

Inadvertently drove by a couple walking downtown and saw him and his girlfriend tonight.

For a year I've avoided all the fun downtown weekend nights for fear of running into them.

And tonight I saw them as they walked from parking a car to maybe dinner, or a bar, or dessert at my favorite place.

And I didn't feel jealous, the ground didn't open and swallow me, I didn't hate either one of them.

Feeling the inevitable is coming — meeting her face to face. But for tonight, I didn't evaporate.

And I wished him well in my mind... mostly because I didn't recognize him from a distance like I always could.

But really, it's because I'm not that person anymore.

CHAPTER #22

Turning A Corner

I want to mark this day. I knew it was coming, and close friends said it would.

That day where I would wake up, and there is no sadness, no fear, no needing to go back to sleep or worry about what the day holds.

Where the to do list is no longer overwhelming, and the writing no longer judged before it's written.

The two cups of coffee and a few minutes of quiet is more than enough — and I look outside and realize, "Oh my gosh! This is my new day!"

Where my head is clear and what felt impossible to tackle a few days ago is only a few deep breaths away from being finished.

Where I don't have to ignore the chaos of the outside world because my inner world is worse.

And the day where I know for sure, it's all going to be better than ok.

Marking this day.

CHAPTER #23

A Tiny Lesson In Destiny

My Buddhist acupuncturist, Diane Gross, DOM, L.Ac., had a cancellation, and I came in rambling about PMS and insanity and choices and how exactly DO you grow a business and that I built a fire this morning because I needed fire and air.

She quietly put needles in. At some point, I fell asleep.

Later, as she was pulling needles out, she asked me, "Have you heard the story of David and Goliath?"

"Absolutely," confidently answering her.

"What was the question David went around and asked everyone when he went to the camp where Goliath was taunting Israel?"

"I don't know." (Seriously- do *you*?? Omg.)

"He asked everyone, 'What does the victor get?' Such an odd question — it wasn't questions of military, or strategy or anything else— he wanted to know what the victor got. The victor got up to half the kingdom... Do you know why he asked that?"

"Not at all," I admitted.

"He wanted to know if this was his destiny; because he was already anointed King by Samuel. He showed up to the opportunity, asked a few questions, and let it unfold. You don't get to your destiny through the mind."

#MicDrop

CHAPTER #24

Finding Joy

This autumn leaves here are turning just a tiny bit of color, then going brown and falling off. There are no bright yellows this year. Or reds. Everyone says it's not time, but the trees think it is.

It's their time, regardless of the calendar.

They have their own rhythm and they need what they need.

I didn't think it was a dry summer, but too dry for them.

I've spent a few days grumping about this. I NEED color. Fall in the foothills of the Blue Ridge Mountains the BEST but not when it's like this.

And then I remember the lesson of the ENTIRE year: Find the beauty in what is.

The more I see what isn't— the more suffering I self-inflict. When all I see is what's missing, the more I miss the abundance, the possibility of contentment.

I'm missing the joy that's here.

So, this year, I celebrate the mostly browns, mustards, burnt sienna (remember THAT crayon color?). I am searching for the occasional red and wishing that the green of a vibrant summer could stay just a little longer.

CHAPTER #25

Be the Pineapple

Update on Jordan, now 17, and his adventure with film school—he did not get accepted. He asked for a reason, and they said his portfolio, "shows that you are not original or creative."

For years, I've tried to infuse him with a little resilience. In short, he's a pineapple— some people love the fruit, others hate it. Neither says anything about the fruit, really.

It's still a pineapple. The opinions have never changed what it is. Our family motto for the past 11 years: Be The Pineapple.

Shock, grief, and a solo trip to the beach to clear his head. A week later and he's strategizing next steps. His resilience is impressive to me, but then I realize his worth is not rocked. He's the pineapple. It's ok.

His art is clarifying itself. I'm telling him, "You'll figure it out." He's learning lessons. Tons. I have no need to buffer, make it a softer blow, or tell him it's ok. It's not. It's a dream lost. There's still disorientation and talk of Plan B. Or C. And Z.

We don't use the word Failure — it's not a recent thing, we just never have. We stay in terms of Lessons, Guidance, and Next Times.

We deeply respect the film school and their perspective on who they choose. However, we believe there is a different place his work belongs; maybe more commercial, etc., and this outcome is a shortcut to getting him there.

CHAPTER #26

A New Year to Wake Up

For my birthday, I flew a red-tailed hawk named Greenie. He taught me that I control very little, but if I'll show up and stretch my hand out, life would find me.

We say we want life to find us. We talk big. But it's pretty terrifying when a bird careens straight for me, with a hawk's eye target on the meat I'm holding between two fingers. I'm both luring him to show up and trying to be brave when he does.

It's in that spirit that I'm not making resolutions this year but working with accepting and allowing — whether incoming or outgoing.

Even though I'm often afraid, every single thing that has and is turning up in my life is so much better than anything I could resolve.

Everything that left was ready to fly. This year will be more of this balance— the incoming and the taking off.

I think it best just to wake up each day, say as many thank you's as possible, love well, trust God just a little, and learn everything I'm supposed to, stretch myself, and go to bed smiling.

CHAPTER #27

Finding A Life I Really Love

I went on a blind date.

After 40 minutes of trading stories he went to the bathroom and returned with the decision that we could go no further because I was allergic to cats and he had three that he was unwilling to "give up for anyone".

I agreed we were not a match, and that I would not take Benadryl the rest of my life.

Then he exhaled, sat back in his seat and sheepishly smiled. The mask released. I was more riveted than I'd been the previous 45 minutes. He then gave me advice that would change my life.

"Can I be honest? I'm really just a shallow guy.

I need someone with thin thighs. Look. Here's how you work this. Do online dating's free weekends. Just put up a photo of you with some skin. They're like sharks, and they'll find you. Get their email addresses. You'll fill your stables for 6 months."

Me: "Sounds like you've got this down pat. How long have you been dating?"

Him: "9 years. Can you believe it? I don't know what's wrong. I'm a nice guy, a good dad, make lots of money."

In 40 minutes he taught me that until I wanted more than a nice guy who was a good dad, who made lots of money, I was going to have to be more than a nice person, good mom, who would settle for money. I was going to have to have my very own life. Who knew? ;—)

I've not dated for a year.

Apparently, there's no marker for "ready" or "enough" or "life."

So… I get to say when -- and it's not when until I have time in spades, and the energy to keep my mouth shut and am willing to get Botox to keep a straight face.

This may take a while... because I am beginning to find a life I really love instead of finding a person that is my life.

CHAPTER #28

When You Can't Hear

Banjo, who's 13, can't hear 95% of what I say anymore— just figured that out last week. It's taken me a week to wrap my head around what this means. It changes everything. He can't hear his food hitting the bowl anymore. Or the door opening for a walk. Or being called to Jordan's bed before he goes to sleep. He has to rely on cues, and time of day, and close up guidance.

Now he reminds me every day to show instead of telling love.

And to slow down and touch. And mean it.

And that sometimes the things we think we're keeping alive are maybe showing up to teach us life.

CHAPTER #29

Use The Machete

Here's a little bit of the good this week. I just want to acknowledge and share.

— My mom calling me apologizing for anything that happened during childhood (all's been forgiven for years).

—She called on the exact day my in-person parenting class based on my book, Momifesto, ended for this session.

— People from another 4 countries signing up for my newsletter for moms (now it goes to 21 countries).

— Friends visiting/ finding / texting me out of the blue.

— Details of selling the house working out effortlessly.

— Going to a Native American circle of women and using a

machete to cut ties with things that no longer serve me. In front of a fire where dried flowers from last season were offered.

I could go on and on. It's been weeks of this.

And you know what?

I'm standing in the steadfast belief that this is my new life.

And worth every tear, sacrifice, and hurdle to get here.

CHAPTER #30

Love Winks

My fault.

I thought this was going to be an ORDINARY day.

But then I remembered this is my NEW ordinary...

Coffee at Ikea with a business friend. I take a random exit to get gas, and a 75-year-old man has to pump my gas while we chat (because he won't let me and the pumps aren't automatic).

And a friend sends me a love note.

And Kolleen sends me this postcard... "This was the day she decided to exhale and lean in toward all that awaits."

CHAPTER #31

Counting the Cost

"The cost of a thing is the amount of what I call life, which is required to be exchanged for it immediately or in the long run."—Thoreau

CHAPTER #32

FearLessFriday

In my grand effort to get over myself, I'm going to post a video each Friday that I've worked on for my blog.

This one is my heart for helping moms because I get how hard it is.

This one is three minutes and done in front of 1000 people, and I'm as nervous sharing it as I was on stage!!!!!!

One day it won't be so hard... (right? right?)

www.TheMomWhisperer.com/About

And for my sweet sisters who are challenging themselves to be seen, and try, and play full on instead of small, I invite you to post something that's a risk for you each Friday.

None of us know who may need it...and it's your turn to show up for a world that needs YOUR brilliance. #FearLessFriday

CHAPTER #33

That Time I Hit A Friend's Car

FearLesFridays are helping me to get over fear, and learn to show up.

The disclaimer is always if I make a fool of myself you commit to messaging or texting me.

I'm sharing this video as part of a countdown on my blog called 115 Wednesdays about J. going to college/ work/ who knows, so it's real life/ real time, and not polished.

Link: https://youtu.be/EnzhE24_hW4

It's long, so here are the parts you can fast forward to:

00—1:45 —How I hit Kait's car

1:45— 4:45 —How J asked me about going to a club

4:45—5:45 — How I took him to a bar

5:45— 7:50 —Update on club and making really hard calls

7:50—8:20—The kinda long wrap up/ goodbye/ thank you

Huge gratitude whether you watch it or not because this space is safe enough for me to share and you are a part of this.

Flattened and thank you.

CHAPTER #34

About Good Friday: What I Can Tell Now

I took Jordan and his friend to a Good Friday service.

Then they needed brownies.

Then as we waited my ex-husband and his girlfriend walked by our table, Jordan the only one noticing. Then I realized what just happened. I started to get up from the table.

J: Mom, don't. Just stay here. There's no point.

I was going to be nice and listen. And I realized I would forever only see the back of her head and continue avoiding downtown.

And here they are.

And I just thought that everything is on the other side of fear and all I want is freedom and downtown back.

So I went to them at the bar.

Said hello.

Looked her in the eye, smiled and shook her hand, "I'm Vikki Spencer." Because when I'm 95, I wanted that memory. That one time I thought the earth really would swallow me whole, or at least my life would. That one time I wanted to stop dodging or hiding. That one time I wanted to face all jealousy, regret and failure in one fell swoop.

We tiny talked then the awkward silence. So I came as clean as possible.

"Well, I've been really afraid of running into you guys so I've avoided downtown for a year but here's the thing. I miss the café, Camino. And this restaurant is great. So maybe now we can just all wave to each other because I'm going to be coming down here."

And somehow that led to them coming to my table to say "Hi" to Jordan and his friend.

And I don't know what they talked about because my decaf was low and I was getting it refilled. I was wondering if I should get my own brownie sundae now, or just keep flaking pieces from J's.

And then she kindly reached over to me to shake my hand goodbye and went back to the bar.

He leaned over the table toward me and said: "Thank you."

I told him she seems very nice, that I have and always will wish him love, and that I hope he's happy and life gives him all the best. Surprising myself, I meant every word. For both of them.

I realized he no longer had any of my missing pieces.

When he left, Jordan said I was so brave and that it was the best interaction he ever saw between anyone ever. I forgot he was there.

"It was my life. It's not my life now." I said unapologetically.

"Yeah. And this one is so much better," he said.

And today, for the first time in a very long time, I'm back at Camino, the European coffee shop named after the 400-mile spiritual walk in Spain.

No missing pieces. No more fear. ;—)

CHAPTER #35

The Essential Nature of Ice Cream

A few weeks ago, I went to a local car repair shop to make an appointment for some work my car needed. While I was waiting for my car to be checked in, and finally got to my turn, I jokingly asked the man if there was any way, you know, maybe I can get in front of the line. Not even looking up from his computer screen he mentions not that day, but if I could come back tomorrow, there might be. I asked what, you know, might work for me to bring.

Man: You got ice cream?

Me: What kind is your favorite?

Man: Any. Just make it good. I used to be a judge.

Me: You know good bribes then. Done.

Next day I show up, 7th in line but I have four mini cups of ice cream (the good stuff: Ben and Jerry's and Breyers).

He gives some to his friends.

In ten minutes he calls me Victoria and tells me my car is ready, here are a few things I need, shows me my 35% discount, and sends me on my way.

CHAPTER #36

The Thing About Belly Dancing

So, I'm in my first ever belly dancing class last night, and I have this surreal moment of "Wait. What? I'm belly dancing? Where was I this week a few years ago?"

I was in a free fall not even realizing more losses were coming. It's the week near my birthday in October, traditionally a time when I survey my whole life, and look ahead, like a personal New Year's Eve.

But this year everything fell short.

I asked a few close friends, "How do you rebuild your life from scratch from the inside? How do you acknowledge that everything you've been thinking about yourself is negative and replace it in a way that sticks?" No answers seemed to help. I'd already been to therapy, tried affirmations, and nothing seemed to stick.

So, I decided to use my birthday and social media to reconfigure my inner truth. The only rule I had was that any and every word that people used to wish me Happy Birthday, I would believe. I had to just fully to accept it as truth – no questions asked. Nobody HAS to say anything nice about me and giving a word on a birthday post is going an extra mile, so let's use that as enough criteria to believe it.

I got over 15 words. No repeats.

Friends offered words like Blessing, Gift, Amazing, Talented, Light, and Brave. I cried with every word.

I promised myself to accept and believe every one of them because that was the rule.

I had to act like it was true.

I had to find it somewhere — even ONE instance in my entire life— meant I could humbly claim it.

I'm still working on it, but the negative is no longer my default.

Ok. Sometimes *it is*. But I'm much more aware that life feels waaaay different when I believe I'm "amazing."

The thing is, you can't be small or scared or inadequate while belly dancing. I've tried. It's pretty awkward. Only when I gave in, and followed the instructor wholeheartedly did it come together. In the mirror I was no longer small, but flowing, and confident even in sweats and a long sleeved yoga top… brave… amazing… light…although I didn't know how to believe it all, the person stepping forward while extending shoulders and elbows and wrists was all that and then some.

What I most want is the courage to live a life I love. Fear is no joke, but I'm realizing so much of it is of my own creation, and I can create a different truth.

So, thank you for unknowingly being part of my journey and for consistently using kind, positive words. And if you just need a word, or two, or five, will you message me so I can return the favor? The only rule is you have to work every day at believing and living it.

CHAPTER #37

Watching What I Watch

We can pay attention to the
heartbreaking OR the heartbreakingly beautiful,
fear OR the fearfully amazing,
lies OR the truth nugget in the lies,
success of others OR that no one celebrated the success of others and they deserve it,
undone housework OR undone by moments.
—V. Spencer (after sleep and coffee and friends)

CHAPTER #38

Hiring A Date

So I'm talking with God about the whole find-a-date, so I don't go *alone* to Jordan's high school graduation next month.

His dad will probably bring a plus-one, and she'll be stunning and thinner than me, and family will all be there with spouses, and I'll be alone.

I chose this.

I chose to be, as I've called it, "Momagamous" and not dated so I could be a mom first. Coming from a divorced family, I knew the undertow of the emotional Titanic of divorce. I just wanted both hands free to grab Jordan's arm as we were going down. Besides, it was a tiny fragment of time to sacrifice right before launching him into the world.

Totally smart move, no regrets — until now.

Graduation.

Ugh.

I've thought of hiring a date. Kind of like an escort, but not an "escort," you know?

And within split seconds of thought it went like this:

Me: So, I really should take the high road, and honor the whole I'm- not-dating till after graduation thing, right? You do see the irony that the day AFTER is the day I could date, right?

God: Tell Me about the dream man you want to be dating. Top three traits.

Me: Ooh! Connected (to You, himself, and me), Healthy (mind, body, spirit) and would make this event all about Jordan and not one second about him or me.

God: And there's your high road.

Me: Meaning?

God: Be those things.

Me: Nooooooooooooooooo.

God: Yep.

Me: And if I take the low road then what?

God: You can. Then you'll have another opportunity to take this exact high road.

Me: Noooooooooooooooo

God: (silence)

Me: Ok. I'm in. You're right. And thank you.

CHAPTER #39

Making It Up As I Go Along

Our realtor just left.

Still much to be done... like finding men's clothes to put in the closet so it doesn't look like a situation people can take advantage of on the price. If you know people are divorced, some may assume that they will sell the house at any price. This is not true for us.

So in the next week, I will be going to Goodwill and choosing style and shoe size of the man that apparently lives here.

Even though I'm not dating.

And I pretty much stink at all fashion.

And now I have to buy clothes for a made-up man that apparently lives with me.

And maybe some glasses for his side of the bed. And a book.

Oooh. And a toothbrush for the bathroom.

That FYI *I've never seen and will exist only in my closet.*

This will be funny one day, right?

RIGHT?

CHAPTER #40

Just One Pack At A Time

So I was in Trader Joes last week, and I get to the lunchmeat section. I realize if I buy four packs, they will be the last lunches I'll make for school.

Ever.

Like, ever again.

I try not to cry. I grab one pack because denial works right now.

And one pack doesn't make me cry at all.

At the register, we start talking, and because you can tell Trader Joes people ANYTHING and they have to listen, we end up talking about Jordan going to Los Angeles.

I TRY not to tear up and start bagging groceries, telling myself "Look! It's ONE pack of lunchmeat! See?"

Ultimately, the amazing cashier says he's from LA, "It's expensive, everyone's trying to make it, he'll be home before Christmas."

"I don't want him home. I want him where he needs to be." I can't believe I'm saying this, but I mean it. My mom had to let me go where I needed to be... it's his turn.

Today although I have five layers of everything going on, I'm reminded that somewhere a looong time ago, he chose me and home is always going to be the space between and in us.

CHAPTER #41

I Just Need Air

I'm bad/ oblivious/ no clue with men. There. I said it.

I'm filling a tire that has a slow leak, but I don't have time to go to the repair shop. I pull up to gas station air pump where a cute guy is standing next to a minivan with two kids.

Me: Are you using this?

ScruffBeardMan: No. Do you need some help?

(Stop right here. I should have said YES Yes, this thingy on the tire is SO hard to unscrew and where do you put the pump??? But I didn't say that now did I?)

Me: No, I've been doing this all week. I just need to get to the shop.

Him: Oh, these aren't my kids. My sister is inside I'm just watching them.

Me: Oh. Are you passing through?

Him: Yes, we're from Rocky Mount, on our way to a baseball game in VA.

Me: That's awesome. (*Stop right here. WAS I SUPPOSED to say something personal?????*)Hey, can you tell me what number the pump is on?

Him: 29.

Me: Thanks. (*I keep pumping air in utter silence realizing I can't go back. At this point, all I WANT to say is "Hey, what's your shirt size because I have to buy men's clothes from Goodwill and I need to use you as a model.")*

Sister comes back, tire inflates, and lesson learned— let cute guys help.

Wait. What if it WASN'T his sister????

You see? THIS is why I'm not dating right now. I don't have time to figure this mess out…I've got a graduation to pull off and a house to sell.

I just need air.

CHAPTER #42

Same List

Last night before bed, I made a SH*T list.

I never do that. Ever.

I'm committed to looking for the good. But not last night.

I just let it all out - all five things.

Then I made a Gratitude List, and you know what?

Dang it if I put four of those five things from the first list onto the second.

CHAPTER #43

Go Hard and Find Home

I very rarely know what I'm doing for sure... I have a lot of hunches.

But I'm taking inspiration from four-year-old boys on ice skates.

When they get their footing, feeling blades just another part of their foot, they go fast and hard.

Then they fall and get up and keep going.

They almost find it fun.

You know what happens over time?

They end up on the hockey team.

CHAPTER #44

Just A Little Brave

Today is last of the school routines, and 6:51 am wake up calls.

I'm holding the both/and.

The shift and the possibilities.

The celebration and the grieving.

I didn't want to empty nest alone. This was never the plan.

But you know what I figured out a few days ago after I hired someone to landscape and bought men's clothes for the closet? (Seriously, best shopping trip EVER. Bought only the clothes I wanted to hug.)

I have a resilient strength and energy to face this now that I would not have had if it weren't for the last few years.

I can be in it all, and it doesn't topple me.

And, if I can be a little brave for one today at a time, I'm going to find joy, beauty, and brilliance waiting for me.

CHAPTER #45

Freeze Just A Moment

Oh gosh, you know what?

I just realized this is THE moment...

…where everything just flows, life is beautiful, it's all going to be ok.

Jordan is still here.

The dog is still here.

The house needs no more work.

I have ideas again.

I'm loved.

There's laughter.

It's all more than enough.

CHAPTER #46

This Little Piggy Went to Market

Our house has been on the market a week and so far, no showings. So I took time today to find ways to intentionally say goodbye. Maybe I've been so busy, I didn't let go yet? Maybe I'm still holding on…

I prayed.

I walked around the house.

I released each room with gratitude and love.

I lit a candle. Because maybe it's more serious if you light a candle, right?

Because fire and matches and you pretty much mean it, even when you're not sure if you really do.

About an hour after I was done, there was a car in front of the house taking down the number.

And an hour later another one.

I don't understand the spiritual/ emotional/ energy/ physical world, but I do think there's something to intentionally letting go.

CHAPTER #47

Finding My Feet

Vertigo— the tornado of ailments.

You never see it coming, it takes you for a ride, and leaves you flung all over the place. BUT.

After two days, I'm so much better!!!! Thank you so so much to everyone who gave me their go-to list. I did nearly everything on there.

There was one point where I was doing the bed exercises, with a scarf on my neck, Bonine in my system, grounding stones in my pockets, sea bands on my wrists, doing the Brandt-Daroff exercise while talking to God saying, "Well then. Finally, I look on the outside like I feel on the inside — halfway crazy."

I'm learning that when life feels like it's spinning out of control the best thing to do is to stop holding on (you know, the whole, let go or get dragged thing).

So yesterday I had Jordan drive me to the grocery store and gave him $100 for his groceries for the week so he could learn to find food on a budget in CA. You know what? He did it. You know what else? I don't have to COOK this ENTIRE week. You know what else? I'll have $100 extra each week once he goes to CA (somebody forgot to tell me about that perk...just sayin'). I asked dear friends from Raleigh who came to visit if I could have time to nap. You know what?

They had no problem with it.

I told people I couldn't get back to them until later. You know what? They totally understood.

I've learned (again, for the 10 millionth time) I'm entirely dispensable... and it's okay if I live like that once in a while.

CHAPTER #48

What's That Like For You?

People tell me stuff.

This past week several some ones' I knew less than 30 minutes told me the following:

They're gay, and I was one of four people they told in two years.

They just separated.

They lost a baby then a marriage.

They bought a place at the beach for their spouse and hate it.

They are 40K in college debt and don't have the life they thought.

They lost 25 pounds and over celebrated and put on 15.

I used to think I had to fix or help or respond in some way— but it happens so often you know what I realize?

People just want to be seen and heard when they tell about themselves. That someone heard them, didn't judge, and didn't walk away— and did ask one tiny question— What's that like for you?

Nobody ever wants to hear "You're strong; It'll get better; Here's MY crisis; I understand." In that moment they need center stage. I never hear people give each other center stage... and yet that's where all the power of love is— in allowing someone to unfold as they can.

I've decided its' really the only chance I have to love strangers and somehow to let them matter.

Reaching out and being available to even the most random happenings around is enough, it counts, its Love.

I can't change current politics or shootings, but I can love those brave enough to tell me their hearts.

CHAPTER #49

Remedy for a Teeny Tiny Life

People have told me many times I appear like I'm brave, confident, and once I was called "smart as shit" which I take great pride in. Heh.

However, it's my tragic flaw to appear one way but operate from another reality. Only a tiny few people know how viscerally fearful I've been. Ok. I still am. Of. Everything.

I was once sick-to-my -stomach afraid to ask an accordionist to take a selfie with me. It's bad. If there is a pill to be less afraid, I'd of found it.

So I chose a teeny tiny life so I didn't have to face the outside world. Or any fear whether rational or irrational, internal or external.

So, I spent time in nature, with trees, realizing they are never afraid and asking God to help me get over fear.

You know what happened?

Exposure therapy.

That's a technical term for Divine Intervention, out of sheer love, creating situations where you have to face your fear so you can see you made it…every loss was another fear faced…But pretty much it makes you ball up in a corner first.

You know the gifts fear has brought me?

It's a plumb line for when I'm playing small.

It's helped me learn self-compassion.

It's sharpened my intuition.

It's a sieve for asking myself "Is this happening right now or am I making this up?"

I'm still learning to show up, and I still have to talk myself into doing things some days (go to this event, place or thing because I need the adventure) and I need to keep pushing through fear...so whenever you see I'm doing something fun or cool, it's because I pushed through fear—every.dang.time.

This week's wins through abject ball-up-in-the-corner-I-need-a-minute-there's-a-cliff-I'm-going-to-die-fear:

Two places who found me said they have me on the calendar to speak in the coming months. Another place came asking if I could speak on the subject of Purpose and I said "Of course." "Well, it's the keynote, so we need to know your fee." Shooting nearly 30 videos with J. for a new concept for my site (and giving up my signature black turtleneck.)

Choosing new photos for my website for a refresh.

The thing is, fear has kept me in a place of being a victim before anything even happens. And the only person that's doing anything to me is me. So, God, the trees, and adventures are all teaching me to choose something else, change my internal landscape, and move through the fear with a little faith and trust.

CHAPTER #50

Thank you Letter To Dads

Dear FB Guy friends who are dads, I'm writing this knowing clearly that men are taking it on the chin in media and culture and yet, it's a much needed time of transition and change.

I just wanted to acknowledge you (as an outsider of your family) because you are part of the solution in the world, and not the problem. I can't tell you how grateful I am for you.

I know you're not perfect, but you post photos of you and your family, of the good times, and the tougher times, and I know you are doing your dead level best and being more influential than you realize.

So many of you I've known in person and I just never know how to say what an amazing job you are doing.

You don't have to show up, change yourself and grow, navigate life with them and yet you do. Please hear that.

You are laying foundations in them that will last a lifetime. For your daughters, you are modeling how they should be treated— hugged, listened to, engaged with, and 1000 other things — and to expect that as the bar.

For your sons, you are modeling how to be men, strong, but not aggressive, advocating for truth, justice, and how to lead without controlling, how to manage anger, that they are and always will be more than a paycheck, how to love their girlfriends and wives if they choose, and what it means to be compassionate in all its power.

You can't understand how it heals women, all women around you, to see you love your kids.

We aren't moved because of your perfection but because we see your heart through the relentless commitment to try and keep trying.

I hope you can see that it's more than enough.

If you are struggling in ways no one knows, please get help. You are powerful beyond what you realize, what you can even imagine, and those around you need you in ways that no one else can fill — no one.

Thank you for either changing the legacy you've been given or passing on all the amazing things you were taught. I welcome this world's next generation as they take the lead — you have invested so much in your kids. I just want to thank you for helping to heal your piece of the world, and for sharing your family with us.

CHAPTER #51

Life: One Cup of Whipped Cream At A Time

It's easier to not ask for what I really want.

Because what I really want is so silly, or minor, or inconsequential. The internal mean girl voice that stops me cold is: *Why bother even asking?*

So I'm at a summer solstice event with friends.

A fully body painted man passes by, and we smile at each other and keep going. I didn't know how to ask for a picture with him. I figured the accordion man a while ago worked out and I could do this but I DON'T.

I chicken out.

He turns around and says "Is that it? Is that all? I thought there might be something else you'd want?"

And there's nowhere to hide, and I say "I'd like a selfie with you."

And he says I KNEW IT.

I got a selfie!!

Last night Jordan and I went to Starbucks at 9:45 pm and I just wanted whipped cream. We laughed — would they even sell me a cup of whipped cream? What if they made fun of me behind the scenes... but I asked. And got it. For free.

I bought one pair of jeans three years ago. I'd always used friend's discards— mainly because I can't find ones that work for me. But I lumped it in the fear category — *what if I'm afraid of trying on jeans, and feeling like I'm wasting money on myself?* What if I CAN find jeans?

I asked, and my sweet facebook friends totally blew it out of the water with advice, and I listened and went to American Eagle. I got the best fitting pair of jeans — and kept going.

Three pairs in my drawers as we speak. I got on a roll... I was at another store getting tops that I needed.

As I was in line, a teen girl behind me said she didn't like her outfit. I turned around and asked what she didn't like? Her legs were "too big." So I asked if I could tell her my opinion. **In this split second, I knew that anything I said to her I was saying to myself.** She said yes.

"When I see you, I see your terrific sleeveless top and your long hair. Then your great face. In my periphery, I see that you have green shorts, but I'm not really looking at you below your waist. You see my jeans? (she said yeah, they look great) I just bought them (wore them out of the store), but all I feel is my 2-inch hips sticking out. You don't see that do you? (she doesn't at all).

But I do, and you know what? Nobody really cares. Nobody is looking. Nearly no one ever has the time to walk around and think about how big everyone's thighs are. Has anyone ever come up to you and said 'You have big thighs?' Never will happen. So, if I'm going to get over this, will you get over this with me? Because I bet I look pretty decent and you look terrific."

She says I made her day, but she made mine.

I'm leaning into asking myself what I really want.

Fear never lets you do that.

Fear is always like, *Oh, you don't want that — it's too complicated/ you don't deserve it/ it's a hassle...maybe you'll get it or you won't, maybe you should want something else. Maybe God doesn't want you to have this* (that one is the worst). But listening to fear has led me to talk myself back into my teeny tiny box with the lid on before I ever wondered what was on the other side.

Figuring out what I really want is a daily, sacred practice. It's building my life one cup of whipped cream at a time. And if I don't, apparently painted men will invite me to ask.

CHAPTER #52

Pulling Threads

I've been trying to practice listening to and acting on my "no".

No to the hairdresser that never got it right... to TV...to advisors and accountants that didn't have my best interests at heart…to jeans with glitter and sequins.

I had the thought last night that when my life starts again, I'll start my yeses. Except my life has started and I panicked because how can you rebuild a life with all the no's? You HAVE to say YES at some point to fill things, to make sure you're ok, or else — the void, the nothingness.

So, I decided to tweeze my brows because that's when I can think.

The drawer where the tweezers are also has my handkerchiefs. A while ago (when I was crying ALL the time), I realized I was beyond tissues and I bought late 19th century handkerchiefs from a linen vendor at an antique fair (before you ask, yes I used them all the time).

For $7 each, I got a story about how these (most likely Austrian) handkerchiefs are created by pulling out threads until the design shows up. Some woman, over 100 years ago wove the fabric together only to deliberately, pull out threads. I still can't really wrap my mind around the craftsmanship, patience, sight, and vision it takes to create this.

It's paper-thin material (which I love because well, aren't we all?).

There are a few dots of extra thread (the yes places) that really make the design pop, but don't take away from the overall picture.

Instead of the whole thing falling apart, it all came together.

So, although it makes little sense most days, my intuitive/ God led "no's" are carving life.

When things feel like a little nudge in my gut, are confusing, not clear, not in my best interest of money/time/energy, or aligned with what I know is next steps, or overall picture as I'm dreaming— it's a no.

Not a badass NO.

Just a little no.

Then there's always the vacuum, the space, the free fall of Now what? What if I'm missing out? What if I'm WRONG?

What if I'm doing life WRONG?

But if I can just be and not be afraid of all the what if's, you know what happens? Honestly? Sometimes nothing for a really long time.

I find time to realize that everything I have and am is all way more than enough.

I'm going to be ok.

Eventually and always on time— the events, people, keynote, interviews, time with J, time in nature, etc. —— show up. Or things clarify themselves, or I receive more information to validate my first response of No, and sometimes second chances. Every. Time.

And what's being woven and designed is far greater than I could come up with by following fear, and busyness and the "should's".

It's the oddest way to build a life but if some Austrian woman in the late 1800's trusted herself enough to weave a whole cloth and then pull threads until something made sense, then it's good enough for me. #GramWasAustrian

CHAPTER #53

We'll Always Have Paris

A few nights ago, Richard Gere shows up in my dream.

The last time he showed up was four years ago. He sat on a park bench and told me matter-of-factly everything in my life was over. Then he left.

Actually, he was right.

I kinda didn't want to see him again, honestly.

This time we're in a park in Paris, on a bench with daffodils all around.

He's doing his half smile while looking me straight in the eye. He has a gift for me.

He walks over to an easel that appears and paints the words, "I will trust myself to learn it."

Then he leaves.

Because I don't get messages from Jesus or angels or passed away relatives... apparently my go to is Richard Gere.

CHAPTER #54

Prayers of The Kinda Broken Kinda Not

All I know is fear never changed anything, but love always does... no words for all that's going on in the world, and in my life and no doubt yours.

Just two prayers on offer today.

I Love You,

I'm Sorry,

Forgive Me,

Thank You

——Ho'oponopono (from the Hawaiian tradition)

Lord, make me an instrument of Thy peace;

where there is hatred, let me sow love;

where there is injury, pardon;

where there is doubt, faith;

where there is despair, hope;

where there is darkness, light;

and where there is sadness, joy.

O Divine Master, grant that I may not so much seek to be consoled as to console;

to be understood, as to understand;

to be loved, as to love;

for it is in giving that we receive, it is in pardoning that we are pardoned, and it is in dying that we are born to eternal life. Amen.

St. Francis of Assisi — 13th century

CHAPTER #55

The Thing to Not Worry About

Honoring my Gram who passed away two years ago. Six weeks before she passed, she was in pain and tired, and we had this conversation.

Me: "Gram, I just want you to know it's okay to go to God whenever you're ready. I'm going to be ok, don't worry about me."

Gram: "Oh GOD, Vikki I don't worry about you. I worry about other people but not YOU."

Me: "But Gram, there's a lot I'm facing right now and it's hard."

Gram: "Yeah but you have a good head on your shoulders and you'll come through. I never worry about you. Your mother, I worry about, but not you."

She didn't have to worry about my mom either. ;-)

CHAPTER #56

Know What I'm Not Afraid Of?

—Women coming tomorrow to an entrepreneurs' weekend where I'm keynoting who may just need to be heard and hugged.

— Of saying "I don't know."

— Of watching life unfold instead of forcing it.

—Of telling someone(s) "I can't right now."

— Of being in a group and hearing negative words about me and not feeling the need to defend myself or even respond.

—Of leaning in to love Jordan well while he's here even though he's leaving.

— Of not knowing how to put everything together but not being afraid to try something if I have an idea.

—Of surrendering yet creating with God (maybe I should be more afraid of this one... but its' just happening so I say it humbly).

— Of letting stories go that no longer serve me.

—Of forgiving myself.

—Of wearing great jeans (seriously this counts).

—Of being seen a little bit.

—Of healing and life taking shape even though I didn't see it coming.

CHAPTER #57

LA Confidential

I try to post things I've already processed but this one is in motion, so it's not tidied up. I'm in LA with J as he finds his life here. So far, we took flight 1993 (the year I graduated from grad school and got married—so, it's like a do-over ;-)) and Uber's Jesus picked us up from the airport.

I needed those winks from above because I'm doing nothing here but making sure we eat and vet potential places to live.

I'm fighting all the *what ifs*, and *who does this*, and *he's only 18*... but it's almost sacred to be on this journey and any one of those thoughts would pull us off course now.

They've already been given their say and been addressed.

But he's putting everything together on his own!!!! So far, he's set up three places for us to go visit — ready to go, roommate(s) included, under budget. He's met someone in the film world who said to contact him when he gets here, plus filled out an application to a store. He's seeing how everyone here has two jobs to make it. He loves it here. It's where he's supposed to be. The reality of him leaving for a huge city on another coast with no Christmas or Spring break, at 18, is visceral.

For me, Los Angeles is SO BIG SO FAST SO MANY DIFFERENT SMELLS AND SO LOUD. I tell myself, *It's like being in a river—just go with it.*

But every day I'm here I recognize deeply the honor of walking him into his new life, with permission, blessing, and support because he trusts me enough to not trample his dreams. That he wants to take on his own life means he's ready. So, send prayers, love, vibes, energy, juju, and mojo as we are walking openly, humbly and confidently in a very big world that really does have a place for him.

CHAPTER #58

Watching Someone Soar

Fear is an easy default.

I had 10,000 reasons why I was afraid this was a bad idea for me to be the one to go with Jordan to Los Angeles. His dad is made for this — patience, traveler, and a GPS chip in his brain, so he never gets lost. I am the antithesis of all these things.

I'm convinced I'll embarrass him, we'll disagree, I won't be able to help, someone will yell at me from a car, "Go back to NC. We know you're not from here!!!" I just KNOW this will happen. But he asked me.

And so we're here.

We came here with the understanding that he would figure it out. Not much I could do. I had three friends I was going to try to catch up with. My job was/is to stay 1000% positive and lay low. Except one thing lead to another, and my friends connected us to others, and LA began to feel like his home. Three people who wanted to/did/are shooting with him. People stopped telling us how expensive/traffic-clogged it was and started to ask how they could help.

I did get yelled at several times— homeless men, and a few unintelligible yells from cars as I crossed a busy street and they were pissed they had to stop. It meant nothing to me and landed nowhere. I just did what I saw everyone else do— keep going.

If you pretend you're from here, no one yells "Go Home".

Actually, no one actually cares about me on any level. I say that in the most relieved way possible.

So, we're here for a few more days then Jordan will move back out to in a few weeks to start his new life. It's the honor of a lifetime to be asked to join your kid as they find their life. It's another miracle all together to watch the pieces fall into place, as he steps into his dreams.

CHAPTER #59

No One Is Like Mom

Uber Driver Stories #543

John picked us up, asked how we were. Some drivers ask, others are silent and I ask questions. But not John.

From some exotic Baltic seaport country somewhere super cool in Europe, John has on sunglasses, around 50-ish, chiseled, scruffy face and he looks like he is going to the boxing ring. He is no doubt a relative of Jean Claude van Damme.

He wants to know how we are. I say "fine." But he asks again, looking at me in the front seat next to him (*because I get car sick- I swear*), he ***really*** is asking, "How are you?"

And after I get over the 10 seconds pretending I'm on a date, I quickly end up halfway in tears talking about Jordan and how we're from North Carolina and J. is moving out here. How we just came back from apartments, and I'm so proud of him.

And I have to let him go.

I'm clearly babbling and stop to wipe my tears and put on sunglasses. I feel silly. Why would he understand? Why would he even care? I'm ready for silence. I unloaded. He didn't need that.

He has 500 people to deal with spilling their stories.

OMG, I kind of CRIED.

Whatever.

I look out the window as the smell of silence starts to set in.

He lifts a finger in the air and says with all seriousness, "No one is like mom. That's probably why I never marry— who loves you like that?? My mom asks when I'll come home and she cooks for me. I'm going to see her next year. (He looks at Jordan in the mirror) No one loves you like your mom, remember that."

#MarryMe

CHAPTER #60

What Goes Around Comes Around

Uber driver story #223

Our Armenian driver was taking us all the way to Manhattan beach, so we spent about an hour together.

He talked about how his wife was the love of his life. How he trusts her like no other. They have a kid together. In his culture, family is everything. He found his soul mate and she makes him want to be a better man.

As I sat in the front seat of the car (again, car sickness prevention), his phone chimed.

Him: "You see this? My wife just left the house."

Me: "Seriously. You have a tracker on your wife? Dude. What about love and trust?"

Him: "Guess you'll have to ask her. We switched phones this morning because I was having a problem with mine.

This is her phone.

Apparently, she had a tracker on me, and I didn't know.

Today I'm tracking her."

#WhatGoesAroundLiterallyDoesComeAround

CHAPTER #61

How To Love A Stranger

I'm a travel wimp. Coming home from LA, we'd been up for nearly 30 hours with delays and missed flights. When I'm exhausted, I forget about fear. Or manners, really. Or editing myself. It's partly sleep deprivation combined with needing just one big breakfast that infuses my brain with not giving a f. That being said, I've learned to take a breath and try to keep quiet, knowing beyond all doubt, that nothing good comes from this state.

On the final leg home, I sat right next to a man who was on his phone, bemoaning that his wife is leaving him. I tried not to listen— as did the whole plane. But he became dramatic and obnoxious.

The plane had a technical problem. Then it had a fuel problem. Nearly an hour later, we all knew the entire story of this guy. Finally ready to taxi down the runway and after two requests and hovering from the stewardess, he finally turned his phone off.

And after hating him for his story and wishing I could hug his ex, (*sleep deprivation and girl code)* I remembered that I was on this flight, next to this man for a reason. (Breathe)

How can I be love here? (Breathe)

So, I did what I needed a few years ago, "I'm sorry you're going through a lot right now."

He glared at me, and I stared back not blinking one tiny eyelash (*again, fearless without food*). The worst he could do is ignore me. I just didn't act phased, so I kept going, "Just sounds like you're going through a lot and I'm sorry you're suffering."

His eyes shifted down, more sad than the defiance he first had. He shook his head and said, "Thank you."

He told me with different details. He's high profile, they just celebrated an anniversary, he didn't see it coming, he and his therapist "had her working on it", but she left.

A parent recently died. His world was being sifted through his fingers and for all his power and money and success, he couldn't make it stop.

I said I didn't think grief and loss cared who you were, and that apparently, she's tired, and in survival mode and so is he.

He asked who left my marriage and I said I did. He glared. I stared back (again, not giving two f's.)

"Why?" He shook his head.

"Because I couldn't live a small life anymore. We separated and then I didn't change my mind." It was the easiest, shortest, least dramatic way of answering a question that really has no answer. Every marriage ends because someone can't go on and the other can't find them anymore. Sometimes they trade places within a day. Ultimately, does it even matter once it's over?

He asked if I dated yet and I said no.

He asked if I regretted not dating for so long.

He had no idea I chose to be momagamous; he didn't know I'd just spent nearly two weeks in LA handing Jordan over to his new life. "I've not regretted it one day. I had lessons to learn. I'm not the same person I was two years ago. I'm completely different now."

He said he could only get out of bed to work and he had to take a trip next week. He was exhausted, physically hurting, and depressed.

He asked if I went to therapy. Truth is, I went to treatment with a therapist who lived with Mother Teresa for two years.

And it wasn't enough to keep us together. It wasn't enough to keep me from falling apart.

And I told him I did a lot of other things to heal.

He got quiet.

The plane landed.

We all packed our stuff.

Unfiltered as our conversation had been, I told him as we reached for our bags, "It's going to get much worse for you, so be ready for that. And then it's going to get better, very slowly. Much better. I promise." In the terminal, he passed me and looked back and smiled and said, "Thank you."

I've heard over and over and just wanted to know what it was like if we're ok with our own suffering. If we don't expect ourselves to be fixed. If we accept that we're tired, sleep deprived, hungry, crabby and not giving an extra f, can we still love ourselves? Supposedly, if we can do this, we'll be unafraid of someone else's suffering and not have to fix or have answers. Maybe in so doing, we can love ourselves and our world that tiny way. I think it's true and it's a start.

CHAPTER #62

Having Nerve

Got fillings repaired at the dentist yesterday.

After the fourth round of shots and hearing about sensitive nerves I asked for a favor.

"Anything," he said.

"Well, can we sthop calling my nervesth sthensthitve? Itsth taken four roundsth and I think thatsth pretty sthuper sthrong nervesth — not exactly sthensthitve."

Got my request.

#SensitiveIsTheNewStrong

CHAPTER #63

Remember Who You Are

Let me just say, with everything going on in the world, this is so, so shallow.

But, I've had questions and comments so apparently, this is a "thing," and I want to address it.

I now have very short, curly, dark brown now, instead of the straight, highlighted version. There's a reason besides I wanted it, which I did not.

Truth is, I cannot grow my hair past a certain length. I've heard about how hard it might be to grow it as I get older. I've tried herbs, supplements, minerals, vitamins, and hormones to help my hair grow long and it just never grows.

So, when we were in CA, I didn't take a flat iron because I was traveling light. I looked awful. LA is not the place to have hair insecurity. At the risk of being laughed out of the door, I followed a few billboards and ended up at a celebrity salon (stylists who work on the runway, Oscars, Emmys) to help me figure out what's going on. I was ready to take it on the chin to have great hair. Instead, they greeted me with open arms, big hugs and belief that anything was possible.

I wanted two styles — mainly straight and then curly for once in a long while. Secretly, I wanted them to go in the back closet and give me long hair.

FavoriteLAHairstylist: "How long have you highlighted your hair? How long have you flat ironed it?"

Me: "Decades."

Him :(*pulling my hair straight up so I could see what he saw*): "You actually don't have a problem growing your hair. It's thick at the bottom. You have a problem with breakage because of the highlighting and the heat. You'll never grow it longer than this if you don't stop."

Me: "What do I do? I'm here to do anything."

Him: "You have got to stop highlighting — we go down to one color. And no more flat irons. And don't wash it every day."

Me: "But then it's curly all the time."

Him: "If you want long hair, you are going to have to go curly."

Me: "For how long?"

Him: "Three years."

Me in my head: *lalalalalalal I can't hear you lalalalalalal I'm trying to hide, and if I go curly, I can't hide anymore lalalalallalal* NOOOOOOOO *lalalalalal I can't hear you.*

Me out loud: "Three years but you promise me hair?"

Him: "I promise you. "

He puts the ONE color on, and I go under the dryers where there are two women. Only one is getting her hair done. She's platinum blonde, over 55, stunning and is on crutches. Her friend is there to help. I'm jealous of her hair. I'm jealous her friend is with her. I'm jealous that she's probably someone I should know.

I chat small talk with her friend and then she goes to the washing bowls, and I say I hope her leg heals quickly. The friend comes back to sit and chat again. She's her sister. The blonde was in a devastating car wreck 12 weeks ago that severed her spinal cord, took her memory and wrecked her legs. It was a miracle she survived. "She's great on short-term memory. It's taken time, but she's starting to remember who she is."

Maybe we all have seasons where we forget who we are... where something devastating happens and we try to fit in, color, iron ourselves into who we think we should be... and we break, and can't grow, and just need to heal and remember.

I go through the washbowls and back to my badass stylist who has scissors out.

Him: "I need to cut it so the weight will come off and it can curl again."

Me: "How much do you need?"

Him: "Two inches."

Me: "Done."

He cut with compassion and blow dried with a diffuser with my head flipped over between my knees, upside down for volume.

Me: "You're not even scrunching it to dry?"

Him: "You don't touch it. You let it do what it needs to do. It knows. You just support it."

Honestly, I'm still getting used to it. (*read: really don't like it yet, don't feel pretty, loathe the word "cute" or "it's so you."*) Still trying to hide most days with baseball caps, scarves, sunglasses, and big earrings. I'm giving myself permission to hide when I need/ want to because it's about healing and trusting the process— and not ever again flattening, ironing, and breaking my own self to fit in.

It's ok because the way I see it, it's already been awhile of just going with it and surrendering everything else. Besides, I've only got two more years and 11 months to go.

CHAPTER #64

If Nobody Stopped

Yesterday, I was driving on the highway, and a young woman was on the side of the road, waving her arms for help.

It was unusual because we don't often see women doing this in the South to attract attention. I passed her too.

But looked in my rearview mirror and saw her put her arms down and cry. So, I stopped. I know, I know —could've been dangerous, and a thousand reasons why this was a bad idea.

Backing the car up and walking to her I'm thinking I can do nothing to help but maybe just get her to safety.

She runs to me saying, "Nobody stopped for me," and I offer a hug because I'm not exactly Ms. Mechanic and don't know anyone who can help.

The car has a metal piece behind the front wheel that tore halfway off and lodged between the wheel and car. She was trying to tear off the piece by hand. "It's my aunt's car."

I realized all we needed was a screwdriver for two screws and the whole thing comes off.

"But I don't have a screwdriver," she says.

"I think I do,"and I'm reeeaaally hoping l didn't clean it out because I never use it. It was one of those small, 10-in-1 emergency tools that someone didn't want at a Christmas grab bag. I asked if I could keep it. Part girly, part kept it because one day I might need it, part don't show anyone because they'll laugh at how small it is.

In fact, all we needed was the tiny 1.5 inch screwdriver so it could wedge where we needed it to— any bigger, and it wouldn't have worked.

She cries again, hugs, promises to pray for me (she has no clue how I need it), and we're off.

Someday, (maybe never) I will stop thinking that showing up isn't enough, that I can't help, that someone else will step in and do something.

Until then, I'll accept that it's ok to change my mind, make U-turns, and believe the little I have is always always enough.

So whatever your tiny screwdriver is for the floods, the wars overseas, the homeless, those without water, victims of shootings or fires or life— give it. Whether its' prayer or a few dollars or showing up or whatever, let's look for whatever is waving us down for help and give what we can, where we are.

CHAPTER #65

Letting Them Fly

To the moms who are shifting the nest — whether it's sending them on planes to college, or sending them off again after the summer, or encouraging them through a gap year, or making new routines because they are living home but going to college, or any combination of the above, I honor you.

We aren't supposed to say much and keep it focused on them, but I've just always seen such a bigger picture of what we do— of the love, sacrifice, commitment, holding, letting go, and now launching in some way.

I see your posts and your courage to say goodbye even through tears, still committing to do what's best for them even when it's at the expense of your own heart.

I cry every single time you guys are posting. I don't know what else to say except, "Sending love" because, in some ways, it's not ok.

It's not going to be ok.

It's completely different, and I want to say that I get that. But love is there. We don't have an altar, a ceremony, a celebration for this immense transition.

We had graduation parties for the kids but not something for the moms, so I just want to say *I see you, I'm with you, you matter.*

I've watched moms ahead of me. I know for sure we'll be needed just in different ways. We're still mom, just more as they need us, as they will.

I think some days that's ok, and other days we just want them back, bugging us through a bathroom door. So, maybe this is more of a recognition of an end, and shift and change and new normals....even when it hurts, and there is a hole, and we knew this day would come (even wished for it some days) but now we can only post a picture and say they're off.

We're not alone in this.

And we did phenomenal jobs — far from perfect, but gut-wrenching best we could.

We learned, and we grew in ways we could never have otherwise. So, this is to say that as well — AMAZING JOB, MOMMAS!!!!

If you know a mom sending a kid off or shifting, hug em. Send a message— or flowers, or Starbucks cards. Tell them you know it's hard. That it's like childbirth in a whole different way— remind them to breathe, that their child knows what they're doing, to stay present, and breathe and allow. Honoring you as you give them to their life.

CHAPTER #66

Because Lightning

I've been sitting with the idea of storms. How the clouds foretell the storm but also are the storm. The lightning is both threatening and illuminating. It reminded me of an acupuncture session with my Chinese medical doctor, Diane Gross.

I came in, and it was just a darker season than I'd known. Before she treated me, she says "You are equal to everything you are facing." And of course, I said, "No, actually, I'm not. It's all bigger than me. I can't find my way out of this."

Quietly and matter-of-factly she replied, "But you are equal to it," stuck needles in particular formations and let me take it all in.

I don't know if anyone has ever said to you, "You are equal to anything you are facing" but it shifts a few things.

It's like lightning, lit from above and within. Maybe it can't even see it, but it lights everything and is the storm. Clouds are not taken over by the storm, they are the storm.

It's still lit even when there is nothing else around it.

And if you blink, you miss it, so life has to slow down sometimes, to really see the alchemy of what's going on.

And then this week, when friends are sending their kids to college, or to gap years, or back to college and all I see is how they are like a cloud and lightning. They are lightning and love even when the kids no longer live with them.

And how I have been learning that life slows down so I can realize it is not bigger than me, to find my own alchemy again even as more changes are coming, to make room for fear, but just because it's unknown...and let it give me the nuggets I need then let it pass. It's doesn't mean we don't hurt, cry, or are shifting into a million new pieces.

It means it's as we keep showing up, in the midst of whatever we're going through, believing we are still light somehow, we will, collectively, light our worlds.

Because we are equal to everything we are facing.

CHAPTER #67

Hole 7

This is a tough one.

At the start of the summer, Jordan and I agreed on a timetable for him to move to LA.

He chose to go to the Wyndham Golf Championship as a marker.

Me: "But you hate it there. I've dragged you there for two years."

J: "I know, but it's our tradition. We'll sit at the bridge and eat and hang out. I don't care about the players; I just want to hang out there with you." *(I'm NOT going to cry as I write this).*

The bridge is as far as I ever got with him for two years— Hole 7. It's a long, boring, hot walk. We sit. A catered concessions truck is behind us. No one sits at this hole; there's nothing great about it except dangling our feet over the bridge. And the food. And restrooms. It's where we go. So a few weeks ago, we did Hole 7. And when the bigger players came through (think: Webb Simpson, Brandt Snedeker, ViJay Singh, Ernie Els) we were surrounded by a crowd and then they left to follow the players.

TV cameras, newspapers, etc. came, and we were talking about their lenses and the 20-foot boom, and angles. Sometimes we even watched golf. I took selfies. I stayed in the moment, but it went so fast— just like the summer and senior year and his life.

Then we went home.

The next day former neighbors, The Parrishes, texted that we were some of many on the front page of a local newspaper. After being mortified (because hair, fat, white shirt, etc.— it never ends...) I realized for all the selfies I took this year, I didn't have a photo of just us together as we are right now as he takes off for his life.

And there we were — me pointing out toward a camera, and him looking. Feet dangling off the bridge. A crowd around us. And now I do have "us". :-)

His car is already on a truck. In the back seat is a box of food, notes, photos, gift cards and blank thank you notes.

He leaves tomorrow morning. He knows he can always come home. This is a No Fail year.

But I don't want him here... his life is there, and he's more than ready.

CHAPTER #68

Finding The Bend

I'm taking a few days off...

A few weeks ago a friend mentioned a retreat center in NC.

Half-heartedly I said "sure." We checked schedules it looked like nothing would match.

She said she would send me the link anyway.

I asked, "Why? I already live at a retreat. What do I need to go there for? To be alone with nature? I already have that 24/7."

She smiled, "I don't know I'll send it anyway."

"But Jen, I don't run from stuff. Wherever I go there I am, so why would I go — I just have to come back anyway and face my life."

She said it looked like a spa — there were massage and food, and a trail, and even a beautiful labyrinth to walk.

Thirty-six hours later, a different friend, same story.

I didn't need a third nudge.

I called, and they didn't have any rooms in the main lodge available the week I felt strongly led to go. "Except we do have one last room at a cottage."

"What's the cottage?"

"It's VERY private, and you'll be alone and have a great back deck that backs up to nature." It's the last thing I wanted. This wasn't sounding like a spa.

She asked, "Why are you coming?"

Honest answers are all I can offer, "I don't know. Two friends emailed me your retreat and thought I might go."

"PERFECT! You'll get everything you need here. We look forward to seeing you."

So, I'm off following nudges until Sunday. I'm pretty sure I won't be posting... I'm taking a big stack of notebooks, my guitar, instant coffee, a few candles, my favorite pillow, and sweatpants.

Truth is, I'm beyond disoriented with Jordan gone.

Beyond.

I can't get my bearings, my body physically hurts, I look "strong" but my heart is shattered and I just need air— maybe their air is better than mine. Maybe I should accept their trees over mine for now.

I'm not a fan of "strength".

All I want to do is find my "bend", my superpower of being like water...my flexibility to accept and go with what is happening now.

But all I really want to do is rewind time just to one more dinner or that Thanksgiving six years ago where 11 of us were all there. Because, although I wasn't happy, at least I understood that life and I don't yet understand this one.

Somehow I think this one will be better in time... I have no regrets, things just take time to settle out.

So, I will be okay in a few days. I may or may not post… send me prayers, energy, thoughts, and anything else.

CHAPTER #69

Falling and Rising

Apparently, I was exhausted. And needed time off screens.

After two days my head quieted down. And I'm not sure exactly how, but I'm sure I will be beyond ok and sooner than I thought. ;-)

"If there is anywhere on earth a lover of God who is always kept safe, I know nothing of it, for it was not shown to me. But this was shown: that in falling and rising again we are always kept in that same precious love."— Julian of Norwich

#LoveMattersMost #JustTheNextThing

CHAPTER #70

Squirrel

So yesterday was Autumnal Equinox. I have friends who celebrate this and I find it incredibly beautiful. It takes time to honor life and shifts. I just asked God if I'm supposed to do something to celebrate/ honor this? More like, "I want to but I've got nothing fancy/ equinox-y here. Now what?"

Banjo, my dog now, took me out for a walk, and he ended up with flower petals on his face, so I took them off and saved them. Found a bird feather, more flowers, and seeds that hurt bare feet. I found a hive of wasps or bees on the ground but chickened out to take it because it was scary and more than I bargained for. Pocketed the rest, went home, made a teeny pile, and lit a tea light from the retreat.

I don't know the protocol, so I'm just thinking of the things I'm thankful for —sweet friends flung everywhere, work I love, and connection with J.

Then I cry because he's not here and I don't see him represented in the nature pile.

I walk away and go breathe outside.

I have this thought that he's not left out of that pile— go back— it's not a feather. I look and its a piece of red-tailed squirrel fur. That's J's favorite animal, and he IS in the pile already.

Then I cry because he's IN the pile of gifts and blessings. No detail left undone.

Can I just say that I don't know how to put an equinox pile or a day or my life together. Everyone just has photos like "here it is/I am/ we are." *But how did you GET there*?? And I probably need the tattoo that says "there is no five steps to there." I know concepts and strategies but in real life, actually doing it is all process and trust that if I ask for help, go walk the dog and do the next thing, even if I cry, it'll show up. No detail left undone.

CHAPTER #71

Live the Question

I just felt it coming on for a few days. I'd buried St. Joseph a while ago and was trying to dig him up because I wasn't quite ready. I couldn't find him. I'm pretty sure the rule is, once he's in the ground, he's sending out signals to new owners.

Today, I signed an offer on the house.

Three years ago today I posted this quote:

"Be patient toward all that is unresolved in your heart. Try to love the questions themselves like locked rooms and like books that are written in a very foreign tongue. Do not now seek the answers, which cannot be given because you would not be able to live them. And the point is to live everything. Live the question now. Perhaps you will then gradually without noticing it, live along some distant day into the answers." —Rainer Maria Rilke

Rilke, Rainer M, Franz X. Kappus, and K W. Maurer. *Letters to a Young Poet.* London: Euston Press, 1943. Print.

CHAPTER #72

The Cost

Since the house went under contract yesterday, it's been mind and heart games of "If I stayed in the marriage I wouldn't be selling the house right now..."

It's been a scoop of fear sprinkled with numbness and a side of "Oh crap."

And then I remember...

If everything was terrific I'd of stayed. I'm not crazy.

I told him I couldn't make my life any smaller, and still I felt no one was happy.

Since then it's been healing and allowing and laughing. And challenging myself every single day to step out of the too-small life I created. I find it's layers deep and I allowed it. Yes, it's a big, big world. Yes, I'm terrified even still. No matter how "cool" it sounds to leave and start over, it's not easy or fun. It's gut-wrenching, actually. I did all I could. I keep reminding myself of this.

If stayed I wouldn't have the connection with Jordan, or all the friends everywhere, or a thousand strengths I've had to find. There would be no farmer, or peace, or #FearLessFridays.

I knew selling the house and moving was part of the price. Because there's always a cost.

I'm reminding myself today that letting go of this house was the lesser cost than letting go of my life.

#PayingThePiper

#LeavingTheHouseTakingHome

CHAPTER #73

Morning Candles Anyway

I feel like I'm in a zero-gravity chamber. With no windows. Blindfolded.

I wake up most mornings and realize there's no one asking for breakfast or coffee or lunch and my stomach drops like there's no gravity.

I know enough to wait.

That this not a new reality, just a necessary passing one.

That the world outside will fall apart. People will find each other. They are ok.

They don't need me right now.

That the word I got in January from the three guys I asked for advice, who don't know each other, was that I didn't need a man and I just needed to heal.

Know what?

They were so right because I'd be using someone to run from this transition like it was a marathon.

So, here's where I am landing within zero gravity...

I'm my own family, and I count. ;-)

I can feel my stomach drop and realize it never stays that way.

As I pack the house, believe that home is where love is and apparently it fits in boxes when it needs to.

To trust my intuition that right now has my tiny life with lots of "not that" but very few "that's.

And although I'm waking up as if my body remembers the school day routine, I'm lighting candles and going outside because I'm increasingly unafraid to sit in the dark just before the sun comes out.

CHAPTER #74

Grateful Not Glad

We had to work together to negotiate a price on the house. Once that was settled, he asked, "Are you glad?" My brain went to *am I glad about what? The split? J. leaving? The house?* So I asked, "About what?" and regardless of the answer, I was already fighting tears.

He said, "About the house."

My brain went to all the trips to Goodwill, the late nights of TV, the repairs, the backyard and trees, the holidays here, and the stone that looks like a heart on the garage.

I'm telling myself NOT to CRY. DO NOT. You can cry in 90 seconds but not now. Just answer him.

So I say, barely squeaking this out, hoping to end it, "I'm sure I'll look back and see that this was good timing." I'm hoping this answers all the spoken and unspokens, and I have no more to say. I cry as silently as possible, muting the phone to breathe.

My head is swirling to the past and all the dreams never reached. And now all the new ones I'm trying to live, each day, and I'm not nor have I been "waiting for my life." Jordan was my life, the house was, the marriage, the work, the meals — it all counted, and I wasn't waiting for my life to start, so I'm not sure how to even answer this. And I'm done lying and making conversations easy and pretending I'm ok. I'm on a "need to know basis" in my life and honestly, I didn't want him privy to that process. It's mine, but it's quite unexplainable.

So now I'm crying, and I can't hide it and say, "It's just a lot." I don't want any response, honestly. I just wanted to leave the conversation and cry into a dish towel, if I could find one.

I don't choose a life where I "One-day" things. I don't placate uncomfortable situations.

I try to stand in my truth, in love.

I've asked myself nearly every day since then, "Am I glad?" and it's just not the right question right now. Truth is, I'm grateful, not glad. I think I will be glad. I've heard I will be. But I'm not yet. I'm forcing myself to be grateful and for now, that's enough.

CHAPTER #75

The Thing About the Middle

As you know, days after Jordan left for LA, I ended up at a healing retreat center for grief and loss that I thought was going to be a spa.

There was a prayer path that went around the property.

I asked for a map and they gave me one because I knew that I would get lost in the woods even though it was a complete circle and all I had to do was stay on it. If you stay on the prayer path, the water appears to change direction.

I asked the spiritual director about the "meditation point" on the map— wouldn't that be in the water?

"It is. Some people find it refreshing and energizing to be there," she answers mysteriously but smiling.

The morning I was leaving, I decided to find it.

I thought it would be AMAZING because the streams were so wide. I thought if two converged it would be a massive swirl.

I'm walking through huge brush, talking to myself out loud because I needed to get out of my head, "You're doing a GREAT job. Just give me two more feet, and you can see the point, and you can go back." I've become my biggest cheerleader, apparently.

I SEE the point where the two places converge I'm good. I'm freaked out about snakes and ticks and I have no need to go further.

Adventure over.

I go back up the brushy hill talking to myself again, and someone says, "Can I help you guys?"

I don't answer because they aren't talking to me.

Except she is.

She thinks there are two of me because I'm talking to myself again.

"It's just me." (OMG. OMG.)

"What are you doing down there?"

"Trying to find the meditation point before I go home."

Silence. OMG.

Long story short, we came up with getting in the water to go find it.

(YES creepy because what if snakes, what if fish, what if everything and I get bit and die, and at least Jordan is in LA, and I was a decent human).

So, ultimately we found and stood at the "meditation point" in the middle of the water. This is going to sound awful, but it was disappointing. It was tiny. No massive swirl.

No dramatic photo to shoot. I asked her to take a photo of me standing at the meditation point. No clue why just believed later it would make sense.

With the house contract finalized, my move next week, my new place settled (locally for now), I'm in this uneventful, but incredibly pivotal point. People are asking me the same list of questions, "What are you going to do?— Do you need anything?— Are you going to start dating yet? —What can I do to help?"

And it makes sense why I, who normally have great answers — can't answer anything with a definite.

Because it's the middle.

I don't know.

And honestly, those questions don't even work out here. They are not in the language of where I am.

I'm still wondering what happened to the safety of the land I knew, and where is the map, and where is Jordan, and where are my dreams and they don't fit anymore, and it just hit me that I'll be leaving the house that I didn't choose and didn't want, except that it came with trees that I'm not sure how to not wake up to every morning.

So, I can't answer what, who, when, and how.

Even if I tried to, it would change, or I would change my mind. But I'll give you what I have:

— I'm staying local for a year. I'm trying to not make any major decisions for a full year right now and all I want is to get to Wal-Mart without getting lost.

—I'm not dating. I'm not opposed to a date, but it's just not the most interesting pursuit in my life, so I'm not online right now. I'm just kind of busy at the moment.

—I'm working online.

—I don't need help (I will totally ask if I do). I actually don't need help packing because Shannon came from Seattle, and Sharon from Texas and Sabrina locally all helped me pack. Jen helped me take breaks. I still can't believe they showed up these past two weeks... and I've been sifting and decluttering since May. I have three rooms to go and six days to do it. ;-)

—I move in a few days.

It's not very dramatic.

It's very middle, tiny swirls.

But I guess it's all about the getting there, the friends along the way, the learning to talk kindly to yourself.

Maybe it's about being ok with things NOT being dramatic, and being really ok with choices... that there are no wrong ones or bad ones right now. That I'm not off course even though I'm off the map. And ultimately that everything is as it should be, even though I will absolutely not see it until it's in my rear view. So, I'm committed to today — full on — whatever that means.

The day I got back from the spa, I mean retreat, I found this poem,
"May what I do flow from me like a river,
no forcing and no holding back,
the way it is with children...
Let no place in me hold itself closed, for where I am closed,
I am false."
(from Rilke's Book of Hours)
(weird ending right? I love weird endings)

CHAPTER #76

Rerouting

Because this just happened.

Because I'm thinking this isn't real.

Because he said he's going to be here to help me move.

Yesterday packing and boxing up everything was so so hard. I can't even understand this.

Jordan is here.

Surprised me by rerouting a return from business trip shooting video.

Had no clue I was moving within days.

And he's here.

CHAPTER #77

Weaving

Just a big thank you for all the love this week.

Spiders are visiting daily now... they remind me to weave and take down, build and let go.

All the opposites held in one web, woven in the dark, waiting for the day.

I'm starting to get it.

CHAPTER #78

Just Enough Time

I didn't have time for getting nails. Since I got them just 3 weeks ago, it was more than I normally ever do to get fill in's. I always just pull them off. Always.

Except errands brought me in the same place as the shop.

I went in— same woman as last time.

I'm nearly done and she tells me her car got red paint on it... she knows who.. she has threatening texts... she tried to wait for police but she had to go to work. She fled a month ago. She'll call police again tonight.

I listen. Empathize. Give a big tip.

I left.

And went back with the number to Family Services, and a little card.

She was already gone for the day.

Everything matters.

Nothing is irrelevant.

I don't know where to begin to help, but as I well know, help is well intended but often misplaced.

Just being there today mattered— even when I "don't have time," or "can't do much," just being there is enough.

I'd rather give 1/2 my furniture, or something— it doesn't feel like I've done enough. But she's not asking for that. She needs safety. And a little bit of connection.

#EyesOpen #HeartOpen

#ItAllMatters

CHAPTER #79

Reframing as Art

I've been working really hard for a few years on reframing my stories and experiences. It's not about looking on the bright side. It's finding a new truth to hang my hat on. I've hung up white washed antique wooden frames, completely empty, to remind me to "reframe". They form a pattern on the wall even though they surround no art, they become the art.

Reframing is an art. It means instead of feeling, "I'm left with all the stuff in the house," I shift it to "I still have all the things I chose. Note to self: Don't choose so much stuff."

From: I hold onto everything for too long — people, places, things.

To: I don't push through things to get over them. I choose healing — and that always takes a little longer than I expect it to.

From: If things worked out differently, I wouldn't have to leave.

To: If things worked out differently, I wouldn't know 1/2 the people on FB, learn 1/2 the things I know with new people, and nature would never be a part of my life. I wouldn't be me now.

From: I've only been on my own for 6 months my entire life.

To: Guess I'll be learning what I do on Saturday mornings and it's ok if I don't know for a while.

I've been reframing hard — every piece of furniture with a story, every holiday, every dinner at night when I light a candle. What I couldn't, I've given away. As I wake up in a new place to new light and absolutely no coffee yet, here's what I know.

I'm looking at furniture and art and boxes and nothing has a negative story attached to it anymore. There's no heaviness here. The air is different, but I can breathe. All that work that felt overwhelming to reframe?

Worth. Every. Single. Second.

Because now I don't only have a bunch of reworked stories about the things I have, but I have trust in myself (and God) and my life… now I have superpowers.

Ok. Not really superpowers... that was the espresso last night at 9 pm that made me think I did. This morning, I just feel that it's better to trust myself (and God) and be wrong, than follow anyone else ever and be "right" in their eyes. Because so far, every decision has been spot on.

I landed the last storage unit. One of the movers has a step mom named Vicki Spencer. It's all full circle.

I was going to say I can't wait for my life, but I've been living my life— putting the foundations down one frame at a time.

I'll keep on.

There is no "when I get there", it's all "here and now" and although I gave up a lot in this move, it's just making room for all that's to come.

CHAPTER #80

Some Things Don't Fit Here

Truth is, I just want everything completed now— the unpacking done, the toothpicks above the oven; the candle wherever it's supposed to go; the coffee measure tossed because it's too small and I have never liked it and I'm tired of feeling like I'm supposed to.

I want to know what Big Decisions I'm supposed to make to make life click.

And yet— it's all the little ones that will get me there.

The things I'm tired of.

The things I no longer feel guilty over.

The things that most matter.

And all that takes time and attention.

CHAPTER #81

What It Might Be About

No house closing today.

It's ok.

I've learned beyond all reasoning to trust the grand design.

To believe it's all as it's supposed to be.

I had the privilege of remembering this week how well we navigated finances together— and how I only now really get that I was 50% of that.

How in trusting an instinct I had on a missing house key created a ripple effect that protected us and the house. I was going to stay silent and in my speaking up, held others accountable in objectivity and truth.

How I realize now I was holding my breath until today's closing. And yesterday's exhale showed me I was just trying to get through to Friday instead of leaning into every day— and unpacking.

How humility is the antidote to expectation and demand.

How trapeze artists trust the next swing implicitly because they know timing beyond sight.

This is clearly not about the closing date or severing final ties, or digging for a sunken St. Joseph.

This is all about surrender and learning about my superpowers and intuition and speaking up even though it's easier to believe it doesn't matter.

So, I'm buckling up, taking field notes and looking for God's fingerprints, neon fingers pointing direction, and friends to hug along the way.

And unpacking in my new place.

CHAPTER #82

New Everything

This morning I decided to stay in bed in my new place.

Truth, it was the first morning I didn't have to get up, and it was just hard to get out of bed. I'd been going and going, and it's all just starting now to hit me. So, God and I had a little chat that went like this...

Him: Time to get up

Me: I know. I'm not going to. ***pulls blanket over head***

Him: Ok.

Two minutes later the doorbell rings.

No one even knows where I live.

I throw sweats over jammies, forgetting about my face/ hair. It's my new next door retired neighbor, Doris, who just got married five years ago (looking at my bedhead), "Did I wake you up?"

"Yes but its ok." I assured her, realizing she cannot possibly know the impeccability of her timing.

She was on her way to her friend's funeral and thought she'd stop by. And I didn't know how to thank her for waking me up in so many ways.

CHAPTER #83

The Last Place You Knew

When I was little, my mom taught us that whenever we were lost and separated from her, just go back to where we were with her last, and she'll find us. Just stay there.

Once I got lost in Hershey Park PA after the chocolate factory tour. I went back to the gift shop, where the really big chocolate bars were and stayed. And she found me. So, for me, it works.

And I had to remember this last weekend when the house closing underwriting had a setback and several refusals from the buyer. When everything felt like it was falling apart, I asked myself, *What was my last point of contact over this?*

The house needed to have leaves blown and the grass mowed.

So I blew leaves for the last time.

When I was done, the buyer came by the house. This is a violation of all kinds of real estate things, I'm sure. But here we are.

"Vikki, I'm so sorry, here's your key."

"You're killing us," I halfway smiled.

"I know. But it was a total accident, " he said without lying.

He explained what hoops he was jumping through on his end to make everything happen. We cleared up misunderstandings. I asked hard questions, and he said he was scared he was making a mistake. I offered to walk him around the property because maybe he felt lost too, and just needed some markers.

So we did.

I answered his questions. Showed him the spring vs. the stream. Walked off property lines. Talked about snakes and erosion and not cutting trees and how he will need the farmer. I ALMOST cried because I realized I was handing off the property in the respectful way I most wanted to.

I'm tired of being afraid of red flags and feeling lost and being suspicious of others. Truth is, I've needed to learn to SEE freaking red flags, and FEEL suspicious of others. It's taken time to know what exactly I'm supposed to do with that besides be afraid. Because being afraid is the default for me.

So I'm asking, "What did you mean? How is this for you?" Because when I understand their side, my side often gets cleared up.

Two days later, we have a closing date of the 15th. No more glitches.

What is ALWAYS hardest for me— figuring out what the heck to do next. Where was my last point of anything that made sense? Go back there. (it felt SO minor, like wasting my time almost, let the new buyer deal with the dang yard work and on and on). But I had no other direction except how I want to be, how I want to care for what's mine, how I want to hand off something, and how I most want to live in the midst of questions and frustration.

I'm learning that every single time I show up in my dead level best, the highest road, the place in my heart where the biggest chocolate bars live, everything else falls into place.

CHAPTER #84

Afraid and Not Afraid

I am not ok. I will be, but not right now. I want to tell you what life reminds me of.

A while ago, I took Jordan to Italy. I used points for a flight, and we did Airbnbs with only one bed, and he took the floor at times. We ate protein bars for breakfast. I needed him to see one part of the world beyond ours.

Everything was great — Rome, Florence, Venice — and then we hit Naples. Mafia level, according to the web, was a 10. Terrorist threat was a 5/5. We had to fill three days and position ourselves for Capri, our last stop and the only way to get there was through the ferry service in Naples.

The cab driver didn't even drive us all the way to the hotel— told us to walk the rest of the way. Graffiti everywhere. Men in suits in front of the hotel exchanging euros.

I kid you not.

We had to get buzzed into the locked front door.

There were black sheets on the bed, and alarms right next to the right side of both beds.

My fear went from 0 to 10000. It's one thing to make this kind of mistake alone, but my son was with me.

We went out to eat and found Italy's best pizza, we watched a street fight unfold in front of us because we were inadvertently in the Spanish Quarter.

I f'ed up in every way imaginable. I wasn't worst mother in the world. I was the craziest. Threats weren't imaginary. They were as real as the military Humvees that rode down the street of the fashion/ shopping district we were in. Soldiers wore automatic rifles.

Next day we slept in late, went outside to walk around, and Jordan culture shocked. Hated everything. I sat with a cappuccino listening to him. Helpless. He was right about it all. I could change nothing.

Long story short(er), we decided to walk around a shopping district. We have no photos of this time because we locked phones and cameras and laptops in the hotel room vault. (Hello—The.Vault.)

But we gave in and walked until the sidewalk ended, and we found Mt. Vesuvius…gelato in flavors only found there..the dock, so we could leave soon.

And a castle.

We went to Castle Nuovo built in 1279, bought tickets, and in the courtyard, a sound system was setting up for an orchestra concert. They were playing some soundtrack from a movie. It was all surreal and one of my favorite moments of the entire trip to Italy. We walked up the grand staircase. Found the chapel. And the art hallway. It was a quintessential 13th-century castle.

When we were leaving, the 65-year-old ticket man yelled at us, in what my delirious mind thought was, "You are so beautiful come here!" I looked back, and he was waving at us. So I went, figuring he thought I was someone else and I could clear it up. Only, he kept going in what I thought was compliments to me. He looked at Jordan in perfect English and said, "Your mama is beautiful."

My mind is reeling.

Here we are in Naples, Humvees outside, mafia men, with Jordan on culture shock, I'm coming out of a divorce, and this guy is basically calling me beautiful.

He gave me a gift book on Naples and called me "Mi Amour." I didn't have the Italian to respond beyond "Grazia," but he knew we connected. He blew me a kiss goodbye, and I blew him one back. We left. Music still playing.

Jordan said he learned more about love in that interaction than anywhere else. "He just went for it — all out. That's what love is." Worlds'. Best. Mother. Award.

Outside the castle walls, nothing changed. But we were different. We sat at the sidewalk restaurant for a two-hour dinner, accepting the Humvees. We haggled for sunglasses from Pakistani sidewalk vendors. We could not change Naples, but with love, beauty, and gelato, we could figure it out, be in it.

I can't figure out this world yet. I feel the threat level higher and higher with each new appointment made to the future government. I feel the graffiti on my heart as a woman. I feel the earthquake shocks rumbling under the surface with Vesuvius in the background.

And yet.

I will find a way to engage, to receive and give love, to not hole up inside and sleep. I will figure out how to use my life in ways that engage, protect and love others. Fear wants me to shut down, but I am no longer afraid of sleeping on black blankets. I just ask that as we face our own threats, let's ask for help. If we don't feel threatened at all, can we look out for others that do? Can we at least be open to hearing each other, without saying we are making stuff up?

CHAPTER #85

Stay In The Room

We sold the house yesterday.

Then I went to hot yoga.

90 minutes with an amazing instructor who is over 65 and her only two rules are: stay in the room and keep breathing.

As we were doing a pose bending backward which I'm now doing halfway, she says, "We never do anything to open our spine on the front. It's natural to bend forward, we're not afraid to fall— we do this as infants. But we have to work at bending back... at opening up. Once we let go of the fear of falling, we open up, and when we do that, we open our heart up."

So instead of strength and courage, I'm working on my bend today. The leaning back. And staying open-hearted.

I am utterly slayed by the perfection of provision and guidance in nature and life. I'm learning as I stay in the room, keep breathing, keep my heart open, and find my flexibility, everything will happen exactly as it needs to.

CHAPTER #86

What You May Need Most

Sometimes you don't realize how much you needed a shooting star until you get one.

CHAPTER #87

Only Always A Flight Away

Today is Jordan's Birthday.

It's the first time I am not with him to celebrate. I sent a box of gifts, but the postal clerk explained the helium balloons would pop before he got them. I cried. We always had balloons.

I usually keep quiet about mom/son stuff because I know his life is his. I'll just say that being his mom has taught me 1,000 things about how to show up, be resilient, love well and that family, time and presence are what builds our lives.

Many conversations at home have been:

Me: I haven't been the mom of a (insert age) kid before.

J: I haven't been a (insert age) kid before.

Me: What do you want?

J: (insert: event, girlfriend, trust, etc.)

Me: Fine. I'll give it to you or support you getting it. Here's what I need. (insert: do not make me come find you, be home when you say you will, etc.)

J: You got it.

Done.

We have been through tornadoes, a robber, travel, divorce, chasing fires and rainbows, girlfriends, OCD/ Tourette's, food allergies, holidays, boy scouts, sports, and moving seven times.

And even though he's in LA, we say we're only a flight away.

I'm beyond proud of whom he is in this world. Not because I taught him stuff but because he understands it's up to him to choose well. Can't ask for more than that— to take all you know and run with it into your dream life.

CHAPTER #88

In A Big Big World

I'm not really sure how to write this, because I know so many things are off in the world and while I want to be in the middle of it, righting it back again, I'm not going to for a bit.

I'm on a bucket list, once in a lifetime, midlife crisis trip. I wasn't sure when you actually did one of those, so I decided how about now?

All I can tell you is this.

They said I got the last room. They gave me airfare round-trip for $100.

And while the world was different 8 weeks ago when I booked this trip, I'm going to get over any guilt or feeling I don't deserve this.

I don't deserve anything. I just wanted it.

I don't know what I'm doing. I just needed to love my life again and engage it rather than sitting in my stories of loss. Those are coming with me too.

But maybe they can be stories of completion and celebration.

CHAPTER #89

Finding Luxembourg

I sat next to a writer and her daughter on the plane to Amsterdam. She wrote a book about saving her daughter from Leukemia using her intuition. I talked about how I helped Jordan through OCD and Tourette's.

And how we both bite our nails.

Since she was a native of Amsterdam, I asked what's not to miss. She said to do nothing, get lost, don't worry about seeing it all, just find the cafe, Luxembourg, and sit.

Americans are always going and trying to see it all, but she felt we were missing so much.

She told me to find Luxembourg and just watch people go by.

"Is that enough to do?" I asked.

"It's always enough. It's life," she said smiling.

CHAPTER #90

Amsterdam Forever

1 — Apparently, Sinter Claus has been here in Amsterdam for three weeks already. He popped in from Spain where he lives. Gifts dropped off soon!

2— There is a cast iron statue of Belle. She is a tribute in the Red Light District to sex workers around the world who choose prostitution as a profession. Here, it is protected by law.

3— Rembrandt had people who mixed his colors. He often made a living by selling other artists' works and died nearly bankrupt.

4— I had ideas that Amsterdam was a wild and crazy place and I wouldn't fit in. Turns out, it's a wild and crazy place, and I fit in any way.

CHAPTER #91

With Love from Cologne

So, I want to fill in some things I've been vague on since we're all ok with jealousy and playing big. ;-)

Around August people started asking me what I was going to do when J. left in September. It was a bizarre question because I had been doing my life.

But finally, I said, "Right now, there is only one thing left that I really want to do. I want to sit on a Viking Cruise up the Rhine river and watch Europe pass me by. Nothing makes sense to me anyway and if I do that, maybe at least it won't matter. It's a bucket list thing. Maybe one day. I can't right now."

Then Jordan left.

And 10 days later the house went under contract.

And I can't explain it, but it felt like my life untethered itself. Everything that mattered to me, home, family, dreams, were completed. Two days later I called Viking and pretty much just asked if they had any availability this year, knowing full well it would be too expensive.

Then I got the last cabin, on the only available cruise they had at the time — the Rhine River.

"But is there a castle and a cathedral on the stops?" These were my only deal breakers.

"Vikki, Cologne has the largest cathedral in Northern Europe. And you will see over 20 castles from the water and go in at least one. Yes. You will go into Marksburg castle, the only one never destroyed."

Done.

Even though I have severe motion sickness and should be saving money for my life when I'm 75. The house sold, so there was a little money for the trip.

So far, I've found a hidden church in Amsterdam, learned about windmills in Kinderdjik, and today, climbed to nearly the top of Cologne Cathedral, and met AMAZING gifts of people along the way.

Today's bonus: Christmas markets that have been going nearly every year for 2000 years.

The thing is, none of us get all 52 cards in the deck.

So, while there is a lot that has me folding my hand, I've got this wildcard I'm riding for now, and all I can do is play it full on.

Do I know what I'm doing when I get home—what's next—where I'll live in a year—when will I date?

Nope.

Because all I can do is tell you what I have to decide right now: Do I eat on the ship or do I go back into Cologne and sit at a bar and drink a Kolsch beer before I leave this area and hit the Christmas markets one more time?

CHAPTER #92

Bucket Listed

In the spirit of all things out of this world and worth jealousy, this day would be it.

We visited Marksburg Castle. It was pretty much a quintessential movie set of everything you ever thought a castle would be: high on a hill, tall entry ways for the knights on horses, massive fireplace for cooking, looooong banquet table, a chapel, and a dungeon.

Then we did a two-hour boat tour on the Rhine looking at hilltop castle and village after hilltop castle and village. This was the pinnacle of the trip for me. It was the PBS show I've watched a million Saturdays bundled on a couch under blankets wondering how I'll ever get there. I was bundled with two layers of coat, scarf, and served hot cocoa with rum on the top deck of a Viking cruise ship.

Everything felt centered even though the ship was moving. I'm finding that if every castle on the Rhine was destroyed and rebuilt, then anything could be. Even better than it was before.

Then through a miscommunication, I ended up at a brew house and there was singing, dancing, and I even played the cowbell for Edelweiss. Don't ask.

The truth is, I've unexpectedly cried at some point every single day. It's short-lived. It could be because of a song, or something catches me as a memory. Or because I didn't plan on doing this alone.

But in the middle of today, I came back to my room to find the cabin steward, Florante, not only folded my jammies but put them under my pillow. And turned down my bed.

I don't think I've cried since.
#CompletelyWreckedWithWonder
#INeverHaveToShareDessert

CHAPTER #93

Not All Ruins Are Rebuilt

Today is a tour of Heidelberg castle (ruins, really) and walking the city. I'm forcing myself to go, but something feels creepy- maybe it's because of all the World War II Nazi history. I'm going to give it a chance because I'd regret not going. But just for the record, it's all foggy and chilly and would not take much for me to be creeped.

Guess I'm going to learn the fine line between intuition (truly don't go) and creepy fear (made up from past bias).

What would you do? ;-)

Went to Heidelburg Castle... learned it started in 1300s and every ruler added on so it looks a bit well, added on to.

There's a fairly large wine barrel there. Ok. Huge.

Mark Twain lived in Heidelburg— named Huck Finn after it (long story). And all the spires really do look like Nazi helmets.

After the tour, we went to an old part of the town where the Christmas markets were and had 90 minutes on our own. I ended up feeling lost and remembering my airplane seat mate's advice, "Go sit in a cafe." It was the thing I'm here for, starting in Amsterdam— Don't do anything— just be. Especially when I feel lost.

A British couple I met from the ship's dinner were in there. They asked my impressions and if I had family affected by the Nazi's. And dang it all, true to form, I freaking cried.

I said yes. It's not the place and time here to spill it, but I had grandparents that were forced to work on a Nazi farm to spare their lives. The woman cried with me- and told her family's story with the Nazi's. And we grieved, laughed and just were together.

So, my intuition was spot on, that it *was* a heavy place. But that showing up anyway was, as they say in England, "laying ghosts,", putting so many things to rest.

CHAPTER #94

The Pub

Another day, another Christmas market.

And cathedral. And snow.

Strasbourg.

Part German. Part French. Part I Should Really Teach at The School of English here.

Truth be told, after a tour, I wandered around. Used to getting lost, I found an interesting building that had a pub. Turns out it was Maison Kammerzell— built in 1429.

Dark, historical, thick colored glass panels for windows, frescoes by famous artists of the 1800s — it was everything you imagined a small pub to be in the back of a cathedral. ;-)

And it had fois gras.

I'd never had fois gras.

As I was slowly enjoying the entire moment of what was close to liverwurst and the smells of centuries-old wood, and trying to eavesdrop on the two Frenchmen sitting within inches of me packed like sardines in side wall tables built for people smaller than we ever will be again.

Then, World War air sirens went off.

Four times.

We all froze by the third. The waiter asked me, "How many was that?"

"Four," I answered completely forgetting that I know "four" in French.

"Ok," he replied.

For a moment, I imagined life amidst a very different world, running for life, waiting for more bombs.

Even now, there are threats to all the European Christmas markets and security was on high alert.

After two more bites of fois gras, nothing happened. No bombs. No guns. No air raids. Somehow that building was still there, and maybe still the safest place to be in Strasbourg, as it has been through the centuries.

CHAPTER #95

Following Cake Crumbs

Today was Bresaich Germany and The Black Forest— exactly where you would imagine Hansel and Gretl were from. The winter here is so brutal, people do not leave their cottages for months. They spend their winters living with and from their animals and whatever they've stocked up. They spend time carving in wood certain pieces of a cuckoo clock.

Each house makes many of the same piece and everyone is making a different piece. At the end of the winter, the owner of the clock shop goes around at the end of the winter and collects all the pieces and pays everyone fairly.

It's amazing to me how all the pieces ultimately come together under a master's direction; how everyone is just basically doing the next thing until the season changes. ;—)

Then the hand carved works of art are assembled as the authentic Black Forest Cuckoo Clocks. You can find them at www.BavarianClockWorks.com.

We also ate Black Forest cake and learned how to assemble it. Clearly, in the states, we are missing soaking the layers of chocolate cake in kirshwasser— a fruit brandy. And clearly, we use far too little whipped cream. You're welcome.

Tomorrow morning we all part ways from the ship.

Of course there are stories I haven't told. But mostly they are of people, and words spoken that help things make sense, and when normal life is altered, what's left is worth not telling for a bit. But I can tell you this: next stop is Lucerne, Switzerland.

Because the Alps are there.

Because in a twist of full circle—ness, my mom was there when she was pregnant with me which I didn't know until after I booked the trip.

#FollowingCakeCrumbs

CHAPTER #96

Wishes Without Agendas

Lucerne Switzerland.

Home of insurance companies, banking, pharmaceutical companies and bread. And Christmas markets.

And I'm going to ask how complicated it is to get to the top of the Alps.

And change money because Swiss Francs now.

And I'm going to go find a — you guessed it— cafe to sit in.

And get my land legs.

And learn functioning High German because the other is not well received.

Because its a little like the Amazing Race right now- to get it all done before dinner at 5:30pm with my British friends who sat with me in Heidelberg.

They were in a bit of transition with moving their whole life as well. Funny how we find each other like that.

I'm discombobulated and rambling because ship life is over and transitions, High German, and time limits are not my specialty. Neither are land legs right now.

But you know what I'm learning?

There's always someone to help.

There's always time to say "I need to think about it."

And with only another one and a half days here, I have to be clear on what I do and don't want.

So, 30 minutes in the coffee always has always will sift out my life for just the next thing.

CHAPTER #97

Life Begins Again

4:28 am EST

When God gives you a message before you find coffee...On a grain bag at the buffet line: "Put your ear down close to your soul and listen hard."

10 pm

Hot diggity dog! Figured out where to find tickets for the city bus AND the gondola, and which stop to take and walk to the next ticket station for Mt. Pilatus (aka The Swiss Alp I most wanted to see).

Heart stopping views and the entire alp chain of mountains is the reward for not chickening out.

6982 feet high.

Apparently, where I've been before, in utero.

And so my life begins again.

Early morning and long travel day tomorrow back to a home that's as new as this land was.

And all I have to really remember is to sit in the cafes and get my bearings because that's where life is.

CHAPTER #98

Normal Is Enough

There was this day where I didn't want to get off the ship. It was Breisach, Germany, nothing notable, I was tired, it was COLD.

But someone on the ship told me, I think it was a captain, that although most people will stay on the ship, I should go out. They use this as a place to restock everything.

But it's a beautiful, small town. Go explore.

I wrote 10 reasons in my journal why I should NOT go out.

And realizing this resistance for what it was, I wandered out anyway.

I got some much needed air without rushing. I found a refreshingly nondescript village. Walked up a large hill to their church and looked over the valley into another century.

This day has become one of my markers.

That I will resist doing what I may need to do.

That there will be uninteresting but much needed normalcy.

That regardless (absolutely regardless) of my choice, it's the right one and I'm still loved, and will still bump into God. And if I don't bump into God it's because He's right next to me, not because He's left.

That the imperfections and failures and snubs and abject mistakes I made along this path have never ever disqualified me from guidance, love, joy.

That in listening to my logic is often the only way I can get to my intuition.

Sometimes I have to wander, with no point, to get the messages I most need... which is going to often go back to the core: I still decide.

CHAPTER #99

Open and Closed Doors

It's another middle— after the trip and before Christmas.

Apparently the memo for now is to live full on but with an open hand.

I'm very clear that for a few days my home will be full of loud laughs, and food. But I can't hold or keep it there. I can just keep the love with me after mom and Jordan leave.

Somewhere in Europe, I let go of the fear of people leaving.... of Please—Stay—No—Matter—What.

So, the image in my mind that is sitting with me today is the entrance to Marksburg Castle in Germany.

It was specifically designed for the knights to come through.

Legit freaking knights.

I stopped a minute just to imagine.

I thought it was just fairy tales but they had a knight's hall and TABLE they sat at, so, they really did exist.

It led to an open courtyard area and the blacksmith's.

But, when knights came through, the doorway was bigger, taller, and larger so they didn't have to get off their horses. The opening soared about 20 feet tall, and rounded at the top for extra height for helmets.

But since 1800s there have been no more knights on horses.

So, they lowered the door to fit the times.

I think the magic is in the doors...the coming and going.

Maybe flexibility, and welcoming, and keeping doors open, and allowing in and out and having a table ready and then saying goodbye and then new hellos are what this season of life is going to be.

It's more than enough.

CHAPTER #100

A Can of Espresso

Last year the holidays were not so fun.

My uncle passed away a week before Christmas.

He was the biggest reason I travel... he was larger than life, and a great uncle.

So, Jordan and I drove eight hours to Pennsylvania for three days for the receiving. We drove five hours with my mom to Connecticut for a burial. I come from a cradle to grave people, so we went. Then we made a 14 hour dash back to North Carolina on the 24th so we could have a final Christmas in the house before it sold.

This was also my anniversary.

And my uncle gave me away on my wedding.

And somehow last year was the ending on top of endings.

This year is time for joy.

In my halfway moved into new place, there's a can of Starbucks espresso, Christmas music, five tubs of decorations from the storage unit and a commitment to decorate this house tonight... because Jordan comes home early in the morning.

Then my mom comes the next day.

And it's my first Christmas here.

And somehow, everything is getting put back together one tiny beautiful day at a time.

CHAPTER #101

Listening Hard

I'm in the post office.

I put my phone away even though I'm #15 in line.

The woman behind me starts telling me it's been a hard day... week... month.

Her husband of 57 years died 4 weeks ago.

The woman in front of me turns around to join in- her husband died in August.

A woman behind her turns around— hers died in March.

They opened up.

They got each other's numbers.

I hugged each of them because I knew they hadn't been hugged for a while.

I don't know what to say. It's always an honor to look in someone's eyes and see them without an agenda. Just let them have their truth. And stand with them.

Maybe we are supposed to put our phones away.

Maybe its ok when we hurt and not pretend we're not.

Maybe it's just the holidays.

Or a little adventure dust stayed with me.

Whatever it is, I know this: we matter to each other.

CHAPTER #102

Holidays Minus Me

Apparently, one too many espresso'ed nights, and the trip and the move 3 1/2 weeks earlier and I've hit my limit — and I'm sick.

So, I've not done the baking, decorating, unpacking, buying of all gifts, wrapping, plus cooking all the meals for mom and Jordan. (I DID do some things, just not all).

In fact, I've had to say more than once, "If you want the decorating done, please do it, here's the tubs." And they did.

"If you want breakfast, all the food is in the fridge, help yourself."

And they did.

"If you want to go to Asheville, and try on clothes for 12 hours, please do, I cannot make it."

And they actually had a better time without me than if I'd gone sick.

I had to let go of them eating at the Ethiopian restaurant without me.

Apparently, I'm NOT the be all and end all of Christmas.

This is a very very very hard thing for me to admit. I've pulled off Christmases for 15 people or more for decades. I can DO Christmas even when I'm sick. Heck, I did Christmas when I had a three and a half week old baby.

But, this year I just decided not to.

What would happen if I didn't push through? Or make it all happen?

There've been a lot of questions about where stuff is, and what the options are, but other than that, everyone has kicked in.

Apparently, it would happen around me.

And maybe even more beautifully.

My head cold is actually healing faster and today feels much better. I'm going to take a slow walk in the park with mom, and let Jordan do whatever he and his friends want to do. He's taking us out to a slow dinner tonight. We are going to laugh, and eat, and not wash one dish.

Merry Christmas———— Happy Kwanzaa—————Happy Hanukkah———Happy Holidays!!!!!!!!!!!!!

CHAPTER #103

Don't Just Stand There- Dance

Some of the gifts of this year ended up being the ways my life showed up as my life....

The million times I said, "I Don't Know. I don't have an answer right now."

The thousand times I committed to getting out of bed even though I didn't know my day beyond breakfast.

The hundreds of times my intuition was the loudest voice in the room.

The myriads of times friends loved me as is.

The tens of times complete strangers just told me their stories from nowhere.

The new ways I second guess my insecurities and failings, with "what if it's not true?"

The daily balance of wanting and waiting, the knowing and not knowing, the Do I Gun for My Life—— or Let it Happen tension.

That healing , rebuilding foundations, opening up to life and staying open sounds all badassery but the Doing of It changes cells, and tissues and that takes time and pain and hidden darkness and no control, except finding the current of yes and no.

And it's not fun if you actually like knowing the plan ahead of time.

On my European bucket list adventure, I met a 75-year-old woman from Tennessee named June.

We sat on a bus ride together to Cologne. We were the only two singles on the whole ship. In 10 min. she told me the three times in her life that she listened to others and not herself, because others told her she was crazy and couldn't trust herself.

Before we got off the bus, she looked straight ahead and said, "Vikki, I don't know you, but listen to me. You have your whole life in front of you. Don't let anyone ever tell you that you can't do something. You go do it all."

In my new life, I get messages. And stories. And success is gauged by love and connection and transformation.

And the marker is not always knowing, but being open to finding out.

And trying.

In my new life, when there are big open spaces where people or roles or things used to be,

it's not my job to fill it, but to wait.

And watch. And know I'm beyond ok, beyond not alone.

It's not a neat and tidy end of year. It's an expectant, hopeful, one... I've almost always cried before posting these for fear of rejection, and I'm still speechless at the connections. Thank you for the millionth time for reading, commenting, and cheering me on as I not only learn to stand in a new life, but dance.

A little.

CHAPTER #104

Blank Slate And Lots of Chalk

Blank slate... no word of the year... no Scripture verse... no resolutions... no phrase. First time in 20 years there's no overarching theme or word. Because last year's lessons were aaaaallll about control. So I'll just start this one with no agenda and a few pieces of chalk and see what happens....

CHAPTER #105

Personal Epiphany

Today is Epiphany... the day the three wise men/ magi/ kings/ astrologers found baby Jesus according to the star they followed.

I was on a walking tour in Cologne Germany and we briefly went into the massive cathedral. Just for reference, this church is larger than Notre Dame Cathedral in Paris. It's massive and took centuries to build.

Once outside, the guide explained that the bones of the Magi were housed in this church.

Wait. *WHAT?*

The Roman Emperor Constantinople's mother was a collector of early Christian artifacts. She kept their bones in a shrine in St. Sophia in Constantinople and later a ruler moved them to Milan.

Their names were Balthasar, Melchior and Casper.

Even weirder — that the bones were given to an archbishop of Cologne from Germany for his help in saving Milan from a takeover by a local archbishop.

It was one of those things that people should tell you and you shouldn't wait for half your life to know...

Now. The disclaimer is, I realize no one will ever know if it's REALLY them in there, however, today millions of people are crowding this cathedral because it's the one time all year, they open the shrine so you can see the skulls inside.

I'm thinking this is kind of like telling who we are and our history and why things are the way they are whether anyone REALLY knows if it's true or not.

But it's what we have and what we know.

And when we're willing to show our skulls, even just once a year, everyone shows up to watch.

CHAPTER #106

Proof

Hot yoga reminds me that we all have our strengths.

Typically, I'm fumbling through, trying to find my balance, taking quick breaks. My outfit is never perfect, I have boobs and no one else ever has to adjust poses to bend to their knee, and I always, always, forget a towel to wipe my face.

I know for sure (like, with proof) others are feeling pretty good about themselves because pretty much I don't actually belong there.

Until Standing Bow Pose.

Standing Bow (like you are the arrow), is where you hold one leg behind you with one hand, and then raise it up and lean forward.

I don't know what happens.

I just keep going, focusing on my balance but in my periphery I'm feeling and sensing others stumble.

Sometimes up to half the room is out of pose.

Not me.

I'm holding until I hear "And foot down."

And we do the other side.

Because I rock that one too.

Eventually I raise up back on two feet inwardly saying, "Oh, is it over?"

And sometimes all I secretly want to do is Standing Bow for the whole 90 minutes, like the three-year-olds who just do their own thing when they get on stage.

And no one is "the best" except the teacher.

And we're all back in it together.

Even me who now needs water every two poses again, and is pretty sure I don't belong again.

CHAPTER #107

Where Are You Numb?

In 2010, I was in a minor fender bender car accident, hit from behind. Without all the details, I ended up with a numb arm and leg and an appointment at Duke University's Pain Management Clinic, MRI results in hand.

The waiting room was filled with people who came in two's: daughter/mom, friend/ friend, because they couldn't get there alone. Sometimes a body part was wrapped and you could see why they were there, other times, and their face just showed pain. Other than a few TV's that no one was watching, it was nearly silent. Everyone in that room was suffering severely.

I finally got called and met the doctor and said, "Hi! I'll be your easiest patient today." He asked why I said that and I referred to the waiting room. Then he said something that I still carry to this day, even though my limbs are now in great shape.

"You're actually my toughest today. All those people out there are in pain. But, Vikki, at least they feel something which means they are on the path to healing. You aren't even feeling— which means you haven't even reached their stage yet. Until you do, you haven't begun to heal."

And he explained how there are things he can prescribe to help the healing start (physical therapy, acupuncture, etc.) but no one controls the process or the timetable.

It happens over time, in layers.

It took months of acupuncture, cupping, and physical therapy, on both limbs, but I was beyond grateful to feel the searing hot/ cold/

pins and needles. Apparently, the gift was realizing that my "normal" state is a bit of hyperextension of my arm. If they just assessed me, they may never have known. But because we were intent on healing, we went with what was normal for me.

What's left is a mantra/ motto I ask myself when I feel stuck, "Where are you numb?" Because that's the point where I need to feel again.

It's why I'm committed to great waterproof eyeliner and spontaneous tears. It's why I let myself cry in freaking Trader Joe's for five seconds. It's why I don't listen to well meaning people who tell me to *move on, it's been long enough, it's ok, life goes on.*

It's why I don't have alcohol in the house, why I've not dated until now, why I've been facing my NEED for chocolate, or work. I don't judge anyone who runs to ANYTHING. Chocolate is not going away easily for me.

But I would like to live and breathe and feel and experience fully and if I'm numb, it unequivocally cannot happen.... and if that means facing things I haven't felt yet then so be it. Because healing and life is right around that corner. It's been true so far. ;-)

CHAPTER #108

The Most Powerful Thing

I was a teen when my grandfather asked me at dinner, over Gram's beef stew,

"What's the most powerful thing in the world?"

Me: "Love"

Gramp: "No. Its money."

Me: "It's not. Because what are you spending money on except what you love?"

Maybe it's naive, or not enough, or misguided but today, I send you love.

Really big love.

CHAPTER #109

The Only Political Thing I'll Say

What I really want to say is this:

I love my friends and family (on both political sides).

I liked the world I knew and just started to figure out where I might fit at the end of 2016. Now there's a world that requires regrouping and rethinking.

That's ok.

I'm not going to be jumping in the activism on social media.

I personally want this tiny piece of my life to be a resting point.

A full stop. A laugh. An exhale.

I'm ok that your pages are what they are.

I haven't and will not unfriend anyone based on your politics. I bless you if you need to unfriend me. Thank you for being here.

Within four years, I absolutely know my Trump friends may need my Hilary friends and vice versa and I want to be that catalyst.

I think there's a bigger world-wide game going on of divide and conquer in many countries.

I won't be part of it.

We have GOT to listen to those without power — whoever they are.

Stop defending. Start engaging. Ask.

Let someone tell you how afraid they are without trying to fix them.

But behind the scenes, I've already sent more emails, and messages in the last 60 days than I have all year. I'm seriously rearranging my financial giving — especially, and I'll say it, no future funds to faith based organizations that supported for someone who goes against every sermon, every verse, we've ever followed. The disillusionment is beyond words.

It's not un-American or wrong to disagree.

It's ok to have an opinion incongruent with what's happening.

It's the most American thing ever.

That being said, I'm only going to say this once and you'll never hear me say it again because it won't matter: personality disorders make for impossible situations.

Let me explain Narcissism:

1. They will constantly be the victim.
2. Never take responsibility.
3. Deny what they did.
4. Explain that you misunderstood.
5. Explain how actually, they are being misled, and your victim.
6. Spew anger and blame because you caused it.
7. They are right. You are not.
8. They know what's needed. Clearly you don't.
9. Disagreement is disrespect.

It's a DISORDER.

It doesn't work in relationships. It doesn't work in a country or on a world stage.

If you are in this type of relationship, know that it's not right. Genesis 1:27 means we are equal. Look up the whole verse.

You are not crazy.

You don't deserve it.

God doesn't hate you.

And, here's the final kicker... men aren't created better than and above women. Men may not disrespect women in the previous 9 ways while saying their women are "not being submissive." This is not love.

I have lost a friend over this political season.

I have had several friends ask about my faith, questioning if I'm even a Christian.

One sister from another thread on social media said I didn't have the Holy Spirit because I didn't understand that Trump was God's chosen. I have had Christians tell me Old Testament stories and verses and explain in great length why all this is ok.

So now it's my turn.

Here's the verse I'd like to hope WE, including those in political office governing our country, aspires to as they lead our country:

Who is wise and understanding among you?

Let him show it by his good conduct, by deeds done in the humility that comes from wisdom.

But if you have bitter jealousy and selfish ambition in your hearts, do not boast in it or deny the truth.

Such wisdom does not come from above, but is earthly, unspiritual, and demonic.

For where jealousy and selfish ambition exist, there will be disorder and every evil practice.

But the wisdom from above is first of all pure, then peaceable, gentle, accommodating, full of mercy and good fruit, impartial, and sincere.

Peacemakers who sow in peace reap the fruit of righteousness.

—James 3:13—18

Since this is my FIRST AND LAST full on political post, find places in your community where people are not in power, asking to be heard, and trying to create change. That matters.

CHAPTER #110

Intertwined

Jordan has been visiting during the holidays, shuffling between houses of family and friends. His last night, he stayed with his best friend Dylan. He spent the night and I met Dylan and Bekah halfway so he could go on his flight back to Los Angeles in five hours.

Bekah, a photographer/future art teacher, took a photo after everyone was caffeinated at Einstein Bagels. Dylan is my soul son who taught Jordan everything he knows about video.

Bekah captured in a photo the pasts and lasts colliding.

Their time together...his last day here.. the last vestiges of adolescence fading on them both...

And yet.

The thing that always strikes me is the light and the connection.

They glow.

They are implicitly intertwined in each other. Focused, calm, and holding their own.

Bekah is just as much of this— her eye seeing and sharing what words fail to convey.

Jordan has been doing everything from working on sets being paid, to interning, to quitting things, to finding contacts and connections, to launching a T shirt, and to learning how to live in a house of 27 other artists chasing the dream. He texts me the famous people he sees. Or a photo of his chicken pot pie he made.

This has been a hard week of missing him. We are waiting 100 days to not see each other so I can get a foothold into my new life.

100 days is so long.

On many levels it's my hardest loss yet because it's an entire season of life and apparently it's like a hermit crab— I changed entire shells.

And yet.

Its light and connection, both. We are apart, but intertwined still. We are where we are supposed to be. We are holding our own.

He is my favorite person on the planet.

CHAPTER #111

Retreat and Move Ahead

I never thought I'd say how grateful I am when someone on Facebook shares a chicken recipe or a story of their child. Something feels normal in a world that feels like it's just turned on its head.

So, this is a normal FearLessFriday.

In 1999 (Y2K scare), and 2001(9/11 NYC attacks) and 2008 (financial crisis in the US), my fear/ anxiety levels shut me down (for months). I couldn't function amidst political, financial chaos, and/or conspiracy theories.

My life shut down. It was too much.

But there's always helpers...as I slowly came out of these dark seasons, the thing that became most precious was the thought of pursuing dreams in the midst of the chaos... that when we're shut down our dreams shut down with us.

If we shut everything down, our dreams can't move through us. We have a unique calling and without us, those dreams and talents also dissolve.

Maybe it's because in the past few years, it's been a different dark, but I've sat with it, and waited. And listened.

Even so, in this round of chaos, I'm not going down. It's all different.... remembering to ease off screens, do what I can, and go outside and breathe/pray/ground myself. And asking for help and reminders when I'm in the beginnings of being tangled.

Last week, a friend texted me that an old campground was having an open house.

I wanted mom retreats there.

I could never get in because it recently went under the state's control. But the open house was an invitation from the state to come and tell them what we wanted to see there.

We saw the inside of the former spring's resort of the 1890's, and just a hint of the thousands of acres, equestrian trails, the 13 cabins. The fireplace in the lodge/ recreation area and the stone chapel, sitting silently but waiting.

I explained to the consultant that I would like mom retreats there. He chuckled. But the young woman who worked with him said, "You mean for women like me? That's my husband and eight-month-old over there."

"Yes! Those rooms are small enough to do single rooms where women could sleep in. And you already have a state of the art kitchen. Can we just have a place to sleep and eat and connect?"

It's the same face I get with men when I talk about land, or a venue, and they realize I'm serious, but WHY?

So I added, "It doesn't have to be free for us. You can make a profit — but make it fair, and subsidized."

They wrote it down.

I'm on the list to be updated, and I have their card.

It's going to take time.

And in the same week my Facebook memories popped up that I wrote seven years ago that I wanted a mom ranch. And there's been no real moves toward this...seven years.

So, I'm moving forward with insight from another friend who lives on the Outer Banks of North Carolina. I booked a small place on Nags Head for an autumn women's retreat. That's about all I know.

Because one of the best antidotes to fear is to find a course that goes beyond the dark. Because I know that the dark isn't "big" or "small" — it's just a place with no light (yet). This retreat is my course.

CHAPTER #112

Hello From the Other Side

The last two nights of my epic bucket list trip were in Lucerne, Switzerland so I could see the alps.

The first day there had a walking tour, and ended with reservations at one of those can't—miss Swiss German restaurants for dinner.

As I walked to dinner through historic Lucerne, open air ice skating rink, trees lit for Christmas, a saxophone was playing soaring notes close by.

It was recognizable the world over: *Hello from the other side... I must have called a thousand times...*

And you guessed it. I'm trying to hurry through that zone, tears in my eyes and — you guessed it — a red light so I can't cross the street.

...To tell you I'm sorry for breaking your heart...

UGH. DAMN YOU ADELE AND SAXOPHONIST AND LUCERNE AND CHRISTMAS LIGHTS AND COBBLESTONES.

I knew I was off—— what's my problem?

I just had my jammies folded on a RIVER CRUISE for petessake!!! I'm in LUCERNE. At CHRISTMAS.

Except, because they have the LONGEST red lights and the shortest green lights in Europe I was stuck at this corner.

There are never mistakes.

So, I gave in. What's the song saying?

I'm sorry for everything that I've done.... I broke your heart. We're a million miles away.

And probably because my blood sugar was low and I was still 15 minutes from this restaurant, I just gave in through tears to yet another round of the ancient prayer I've been working with for a year... I'm so sorry. Thank you. I forgive you. I love you (but not like that, just love).

Green light.

Amazing dinner and meandering of Old Towne Lucerne.

Back home.

Bed time.

It was a long day.

The next day was an early start to the top of the alps.

As previously explained, my full circle of life because my mom was pregnant with me when she visited the same summit.

Return to Lucerne and made arrangements with friends to meet them for dinner.

So, until 7 pm, I wandered Lucerne's cobblestone streets, stunning lights, and fluffy faux furs on outdoor seats at coffee shops.

I ended up at the same street corner to get to the spot for dinner.

Same saxophonist.

Same song. (I kid you not).

Same red light — that changed quickly to green.

I must have tried a thousand times to tell you I'm sorry...

And I stayed and listened. No more glitches. No tears. Like everything was just settled. I tossed Swiss francs in the guitar case. He smiled. I smiled back. I walked toward dinner.

In front of the opera building there was a band playing (like an army band) dressed up as aliens from a Star Wars cantina (I don't ask) ... their song? Toto's "Love Isn't Always On Time".

I can't hurry healing and I don't know how it works except to keep showing up to all the layers and all the feels.

One day, it will be to love.

But not yet.

I can feel huge movement toward being ready, but I clearly see a few final touches and shifts I'm addressing. ;-)

*Edited: At this point, two months later, I can tell you I have never again heard Adele's "Hello."

***Edited: It's now two years later, I've still never heard it.*

CHAPTER #113

Blind Date with a Book

Valentine's Day is my least favorite holiday ever. It doesn't even matter why. Suffice it to say, I spent 18 years coloring the milk pink as a "family tradition" and feeling like that was enough to celebrate.

But this year I'd found a bookstore in Asheville, NC that had a whole wall of books wrapped in brown paper bags. The wall read: "Blind Date With A Book". Think speed dating with words.

The wall instructed the very brave to choose a book without knowing anything except a few adjectives of the promise of what you get should you choose it…

#1— "Dark, Tall, Flights of Fancy"

#2— "Adventurous, Nature, Romantic, Home "

#3— "Murderous, Mysterious, Coming of Age, Divine "

#4 — "Expensive, Luxury, Adventurous, Romantic"

So, I chose book #2 and #3.

Never a fan of fiction, I don't even know why I chose two books.

But this year Jordan's friend Kait, who was oddly without a date or boyfriend, suggested we hang out for Valentine's Day since being alone would be worse than no pink milk. Besides, we both missed Jordan.

So we adventured to Chapel Hill, NC for Asian food.

I told her about my day trip to Asheville and bragged about the books and the date I had waiting for me at home after she and I were done with dinner; *Animal Dreams* by Barbara Kingsolver.

Then I gave her own Blind Date book: *Murderous, Mysterious, Coming of Age, Divine*

She opened *The Clay Girl* by Heather Tucker and read the back cover. Kait was already wearing a coral and orange outfit that matched the coral seahorse on the cover. It would become one of her favorites of all time.

We laughed, talked intuition, men, travel, and invariably, Kait tossed a pearl of hard won wisdom: "You are what you love, not who loves you."

On the drive home, out of the blue, Jordan called my phone and we three laughed and talked about our celebrations even though we were far away. Somewhere between *Animal Dreams* and *The Clay Girl*, we didn't even miss the pink milk.

CHAPTER #114

So We Talked

I took Banjo, my part Irish Wolfhound dog, to the vet this week— all normal yearly stuff.

I haven't talked about him much because partly, I've struggled with feeling "stuck" with him, partly taking him for granted, and partly needing him more than I can acknowledge.

He is not the second child I never had.

But he is my reason to get up every morning.

And get outside and walk three times a day.

And remember to eat.

At the vet's we started talking about his mobility and how his back legs are failing at times. He has knee, hip and back pain. He'll be 15 on April 1 which is just a day we made up so we could remember. He's 105 dog years now.

She said he's three years older than she usually sees with 60lb. dogs.

I just tell her I needed him.. It's been a little chaotic.

She says he's lost 6 pounds since September was that intentional?

I explain life since September— the new place and leashed walks, maybe he misses Jordan.

She says how it looks like he's hanging in there for me although he's in pain.

Of course I'm in tears.

We talk pain management options. Small doses of morphine should help. But I know there's another talk to be had because I had it with my Gram and Uncle John.

So that night and every night since Banjo and I talk. I massage his hips and rub his belly. We talk about the time we got him… and how he chased rabbits and squirrels. How he was the therapy dog when Jordan had OCD...how he made it 15 hours when we moved... how he humbly stood between me and anyone yelling at me...how he hid when I was the one yelling… how his bark at things in the night kept me safe.

How he can go whenever he needs to because I don't want him to hurt.

How at some point I'm asking him to let me know when he's done and we'll walk this road together.

He licks my head every night when I tell him, "It wasn't today. I'm so glad you're here. I'm ok without you. Not really but I will learn to be. Thank you for being here."

I was just starting a new daily routine... but now it includes walks and a park and before bed forehead kisses.

I am dearly learning to not overlook the things I take for granted... to lean into imminent loss, to thank out loud even and especially when it looks crazy to do it. That I used to not realize fully all the pieces of my life and now I can't miss them.

And that I don't control so many variables but I can love and have very few regrets.

CHAPTER #115

Maybe This Is All We Really Need

Deep Listening is a Superpower.

CHAPTER #116

- 10 -

10 Beautiful Things About Life Now

1) My friend Jennifer has a once a month gathering.

2) My neighbor, Lisa said Mr. Apples the local tabby cat sits under my car most days.

3) I still have nature—— earth, starry sky, and water within a short walk of my home. Oh. And sunsets.

4) A neighbor left a gift book for me on my doorstep last night.

5) Banjo was in the emergency room last week and my great friend Sabrina helped me get him there. But by the next morning he was 90% better and they refunded me $100!

6) I am starting to be ok in my new life. Alone but not lonely, realizing that if there's no chocolate stash, no one took it but me...

7) The farmer texted me *Hello.* I texted *Hello* back. I bet he misses me.

8) Its ok to not know stuff, to be wrong, but I have to try. It's easier to say this that than to do it.

9) I have a few irons in the fire... just learning that they aren't the center of life but a part of a bigger picture.

10) Dating will happen this year. Just not yet. Starting to sort myself into my very own, shiny, new world that I absolutely love....so that I don't need to get swallowed up in someone else's.

Thank you, as always, for reading...there's no five steps to doing life, so I'm ok with realizing that enough two steps up and one step back means I'm dancing.

CHAPTER #117

Taking A Break

A little heads up....

I'll be taking a social media sabbatical for at least 30 days.

When friends I love post "I'm off FB" I'm like "NOOOOOOOOO Don't leave me here!!!! "

But I'm not deleting my account.

I'm not isolating and I absolutely will be back.

All I can tell you is in January, I was encouraged to grieve and now I'm being encouraged to Heal. Like every last bit.

I'm overhauling everything including food because apparently chocolate isn't a food group. Brutal truth.

I expect withdrawals, cold sweats, anxiety and feeling like I'm falling without Facebook and all screens (no news, no social media, no TV). But that's part of the process.

So I promise to not do anything fun or adventurous (nothing planned!!) if you promise to be here when I get back.

Or I'll message you.

And bug you.

(If you see posts on my business page, they've been scheduled...)

CHAPTER #118

XOXO

Ok...so this is it for at least 30 days...just needing to find my soul legs without the static...

I wanted to leave you with a thank you — for being my friends here, for helping me through fear, for endless cheering on as I was figuring out a new way of being.

Because if you taught me anything, you taught me that it's a little crazy to hide and there might be a little amazingness to life and the whole time I'm like YOU are amazing and awesome.

XOXOXOXOXOXO x 10 million

CHAPTER #119

10 Weeks: Part 1

Thirty days turned into 10 weeks.

I had become addicted to screens and needed time off to live in the 3D world.

I needed to face the reality of life without anything to run to: no men, no substances, no screens, no news, no social media, no TV.

There was, however, chocolate.

CHAPTER #120

10 Weeks: Part 2

I have never talked about my life in the 10 weeks I "disappeared."

Partly because I have never wanted to be judged.

For being in absolute pieces.

For being more than willing to force my life into being. To drive myself into the ground to make life work. But instead working with Heather, a professional therapist, that asked me to do neither.

But to wait.

And be.

And show up to counseling every. single. week.

"That's bullshit. I've never just *done nothing* in my whole life. I go hard, I plan. I make things happen. What was last month about with all the grieving? I thought this month we move forward," I finally felt emotion – anger.

"This month you heal," she offered.

"What was last month?" I demanded.

"Grieving," she replied looking me in the eye.

"Let me guess. Not the same thing?" I'm sure my eyebrow was cocked and I'm betting my head tilted in the smart ass way that happens when I'm snarky but trying to be polite.

"It can be. But healing is different," she stayed steady.

She asked me to get off screens for four weeks. I told her I'd think about it. I wasn't going offline. It was all I had left to the world – my facebook friends, FearLessFridays, my website, news.

I was going to prove her wrong and push through and sell the 55 videos for moms I made with Jordan — just as soon as I could figure out what to say. I came back the next week with no ability to move forward. No post on the mom blog. No words for a sales page. No brain space to lead a course. Nothing.

My online business required stories of family and quirky interactions and parenting wins.

That season was over.

I didn't even know how to market my parenting book, *Momifesto*, anymore.

I asked for another week before the Big Switch Off Screens threat. If I could make headway, then she was incorrect, and I could stay online.

I switched gears. I thought about a resume — several years of experience running a packaging company, logistics, accounts receivable and payable, and customer service. But all the contacts I had were his business contacts, none of my own.

Undeterred, I thought about a part time job. One tiny problem. I had yet to go 24 hours without breaking down crying. I could get through an interview but not even half a day.

Every avenue I thought of came to a complete halt.

After two weeks of being committed to healing by pressing ahead, picking myself up and figuring life out, I was no longer ok.

I had put so many strategies in place- how could this FAIL?

As a coach I know the body, mind, soul connection… I locked my thoughts on getting through, being positive, looking for the opening; I showed up for acupuncture and/ or energy work; I worked out; did hot yoga; engaged in prayer and meditation, EFT (Emotional Freedom Technique) tapping, journaling, gratitude, and forgiveness until I had no one left to forgive. I talked to trees. I went for walks. I adventured across the globe.

It was supposed to "work".

But loss and grief are untamed adventures.

There is no contract they make with us, no promise of *If I go through all the right motions, then the deal is Life shows up.*

It's actually a whole new world, new landscape and deserves more respect than ever thinking we can behaviorally engineer our experience of it.

Facing my worst fear yet, in tears in Heather's office, I admitted my inability to help myself. I could no longer push my life forward. I'd been pushing all the buttons on the control panel I had- nothing connected anymore.

Heather, diagnosed me with complex-post-traumatic stress (cPTSD). It had all been too much.

I was officially in survival mode.

Aware of it or not, my brain was trying to protect me from more losses which were translating subconsciously as trauma. No moving forward because forward is dangerous.

It's fear on steroids trying to save my life.

I immediately rejected her diagnosis, "I don't understand. I've not been in war or a victim of a crime. I've had some losses — big deal. This diagnosis, this concept is so extreme."

But we recounted everything that happened in a time frame too short to grieve, with full attention, each loss. Everything I'd ever been afraid of losing, and built my life around, was gone within two and a half years.

—Jordan and I had been through a tornado that destroyed the nature that was my solace.

—I navigated through dissecting apart an almost 19 year marriage when we built our world around family.

—I said goodbye to my grandmother, my person in the world, when I took for granted she would always be on the other end of the phone giving me the recipe for the Autumn Apple Cake.

— I said goodbye to my Uncle, my other person in the world, whose birthday was the day after mine, my Godfather who I told via Face Time, I was returning to God.

— I said goodbye to two friends who moved out of state when all I wanted to do was beg them to stay.

— I said goodbye to a business that dictated the routine of our family for 10 years, and mine for three, now leaving me with a vacuum of open days.

— I said goodbye to Jordan, my son who, with my blessing and support, chased dreams in Los Angeles instead of staying local for college.

— I said goodbye to the log home on two acres. For six years, the most stable home I'd had in the last 15 years.

—— I said goodbye to three sister friends who each left over misunderstandings and chasms too big to repair during a season of so much pain for me.

— I said goodbye to promoting my book and my online business. I had no stories left to offer, nor compassion to give those struggling.

— I said goodbye to my hair. As shallow as it sounds, looking in the mirror every day was a practice in accepting I didn't know myself or my life anymore.

— I said goodbye to dating, with nothing to offer, it was best to not grab onto men who would be glad to have me, but for all the wrong reasons.

—Banjo was winding down in front of me. We already began talking about letting him go. He had gotten me so far.

Heather told me the words I most needed to hear, "It's not your fault."

"It is my fault." I was matter of fact and stoic, taking it on the chin.

"It's not. You didn't do all this," the compassion nearly whispered.

"I totally did all this," now with tears of guilt, shame, helplessness and complete responsibility for everything that could have never entirely depended on me.

"It's not. You didn't," she shook her head slowly.

"But it's mine to fix. And to pull myself up and make my life work again. You're asking me to do NOTHING. I Don't.Do. Nothing," it was the final shred of control I had and I wasn't letting go.

Every strategy I used was supposed to "work." Strategies are to rebuild patterns, habits, and lives. How could this not pull me out when I'd seen so many others change their whole world?

Because when it comes to even one loss, science doesn't agree with self-help $99 courses and 10 Steps to Putting Your Life Back Together outlines.

One loss triggers a primal survival instinct in the brain. Memory is the first to go. Then, brain fog ensues. Up to 30% of brain capacity can be lost as the body shifts into physically surviving what it sees as a threat. Because life was so incredibly communal for humans, any loss triggers very deep and subconscious fears of isolation. Isolation meant death. In short, if you're a part of a community, routine, work – you're safe. Without even one of those, your brain thinks your survival is in danger.

I also learned losses are cumulative. Each fresh loss triggers any unresolved bits from the last one(s).

"Bits" is the incredibly technical term.

This is why it's hard to get on top of loss through going through all the strategies you would normally use with daily stress.

How long it takes to move through, how quickly, how efficiently, is a mystery.

My stance was to face it head on.

My expectation was to keep functioning without medication and engage in life.

But it didn't happen that way.

I didn't expect the antigravity — everything that held me together and that I orbited around was gone.

So now what? I wanted the Five Step Plan for moving on in 30 days or less and living your dream life.

I was in. What could I not muscle through?

Heather was not having my plan.

" I'm asking you to give the attention you've given to others to yourself. You sleep. You get up. Make coffee. Sit. Journal. Go take a walk. Come back and read. Start to make lunch for yourself. Eat lunch. Go take a bath. Take a nap. I think you'll find that intentionally taking care of yourself takes time."

"That's such bull." I was disoriented, humiliated.

I was embarrassed that I wasn't strong or smart or brave enough to push through this season of life and make it work. Get a 9 to 5. Pick myself up. I didn't want to rely on an alimony check. I didn't trust on any level that a few naps were my golden ticket out of cPTSD.

Heather asked, "Imagine a young girl who has just been brought by social services and has been in crisis. What would you do for her?"

I knew this one. "I'd hug her, and give her food, and let her sleep, and tell her she's safe. I'd stay with her until she could get help and feel safe and keep people away. I'd let her walk outside or play with crayons, whatever she wanted."

Heather replied, "Would you blame her for coming to you? Is her situation her fault?"

Me, totally not getting it, "Absolutely not."

Heather connected all the pieces, "That's what I need you to do for yourself."

Instantaneously crystal clear on the situation, I crumpled in the chair in a pile of cries that I don't remember ever crying before. It felt like every loss could finally release the devastation it carried…the hole it left… every.single. loss.

I needed to fall apart without trying to save myself any more. I needed to stop being afraid to face being broken.

So, I shattered.

CHAPTER #121

10 Weeks: Part 3

Grief and healing reminds me of childbirth.

I'm in it, but not controlling it. I'm in pain, and confused and have no timetable for when it will stop or how much more it will hurt. My best bet is to go with it because the bet was, it knew exactly what to do.

3:20 am — Wake up and can't get comfortable; can't fall asleep; can't stay awake. Everything hurts.

3:45 am — A bath might help. Ignore the time. Light candles. Breathe. Maybe I just needed to breathe.

4:25 am — Exhaustion sets in, attempt at sleep, propping pillows wherever they feel good.

5:15 am — Dreams stop and eyes open, forget this is the new bedroom, pretend it's not happening, where's Jordan, breathe, feel it all, allow the reality to set in again. Go to the bathroom and look in the mirror, remember it all got cut off, and wherever it ended up is the same area where Jordan is.

Finally agree it can swallow you whole. Just be done.

But it never does.

Life is trying to find a new rhythm by shredding the old one.

Tomorrow is better. Naps for an hour feel like a lifetime.

Days go by- some repeating the all- night schedule, others start to cadence into longer stretches of night and day.

Life stabilizes into breath, tears, allowing, walks.

And nothing is actually swallowing you whole — even when you wish it would.

CHAPTER #122

10 Weeks: Part 4

Every ounce of my upbringing said I was blatantly wasting my life. I journaled cuss words of how horrible of a human being I am for taking a second bath that day because I didn't know what else to do. There was no social media to show pictures of my feet dangling in a tub of water saying, "Bath #2 today! Wish me luck!"

I hated giving in to "doing nothing" — eating, sleeping, cleaning, walking the dog, driving just to drive, reading, joining the neighbors' book club, showing up to the Native American women's circle, joining a friend at acting classes, going to her home to eat dinner, drives to my dad and step mom's house, dinners with Jordan's friends Bekah and Dylan.

Everything was surreal.

It was too easy. It wasn't "enough".

I wasn't "earning" my keep. I wasn't "earning" my life. What was I good for?

Apparently, with grief, loss, healing, there is nothing to fix because even in this, I am not broken.

I am hurting.

There is nothing to earn; worth, value, deserving of love – it's all that's left that refuses to leave.

It gives just enough strength to make the coffee.

If I had a dime every time I heard, "You look like you're doing great…you're so strong… " I'm never sure what to say.

So, here's what I really want to say but am too polite to speak out loud…

"Hi, yeah, thanks for coming over. So, here's the thing. I've got 1000 pieces of my life on the floor here--yeah, no lights or windows, I know. Hey, can you help me find the fucking border pieces? Just feel for them. We've got to start somewhere, right?

So sorry about your lost keys, and your latte they got wrong… Mind handing me a tissue while I babble about random pieces of life while we keep feeling for the edge pieces?

Can you not leave to make dinner for your family since it leaves me here alone? Or at least take me with you? I've been eating alone for two straight weeks and recently skipping dinner because I can't eat a whole chicken pot pie without crying.

I also don't know what to do with the ten dinner plates I have.

What do I do with so many plates?

Yeah, so I did get a speeding ticket. And, I read a little.

Did you find a border piece yet? Me neither.

Yeah, I know, this new place is beautiful isn't it? But I still can't remember where my coffee grinder is in the morning. And no one is here to make breakfast for, and I don't remember what I used to eat.

No, I can't make lasagna because that was his birthday favorite and the pork chops were for winter days only because they go in the crock pot.

You can just keep looking for these border pieces. They have to be here somewhere, right? I mean, no border pieces, what are we left with?

I know, I know, I need to go to church. Trust God. Walk in faith. Thanks for the Bible verse. Here's the thing. You know Psalm 23 talks about the Valley of the Shadow of Death?

Well whatever place is in the actual valley and not just the shadow, I'm there. So, that verse doesn't apply. I just figured God was big enough to be here too beyond the verses, and beyond faith. Don't you think?

I'm so glad you got a few Christmas gifts on sale, and your 401K is doing well, and you found coupons for the rotisserie chicken and water park for the summer. Can I ask you a question?

What's broken you to the core lately? Not pissed you off, for wrecked your coffee. What's Broken. Your. Heart?

And how are you coming to terms with that?

Because here's the thing.

Right now, the only people who can walk with me are the ones who have been shattered and have had to learn to love the pieces, even the ones they can never pick up again.

Find any border pieces yet?

Me neither. "

CHAPTER #123

10 Weeks: Part 5

It took weeks, but in time, I was aware of being thirsty. Or truly tired. Or when I sat outside, I heard the birds' wings against the air as they flew overhead.

No longer in overdrive, I wasn't responding to the next emergency, or crisis, or need that someone else had. I was very very good at handling all that. What I needed help with was listening to my own life and world.

In time, I put pieces of paper on the walls with no expectations or agenda. Colored markers waited in a pile. I did this earlier in the year, but nothing came – no ideas, no to do lists, it was like my mind was as empty as the paper.

But I wanted to try again.

This time, I put up 12 smaller pieces of paper on a large IKEA closet that I helped put together a few years ago. Maybe it could help put me together now.

I had no rules, just anything I wanted. For a few days I added nothing.

Finally, I drew a dot on the 3rd paper: "Graduated high school — 1987."

Then another dot on the 4th paper: "Graduated college—1993, Masters."

Ooh. Almost forgot: "Graduated college — 1991, BA in English, with secondary education certification. Heh. "

Hey… "Book published: 2014"

And on it went. Disjointed but flowing.

The gifts, family memories, life pivots, awards, moves we made, trajectories all mapped became points of contact to life.

No one could take these away.

Because they were points that already happened, and were no threat of loss. I flew under my own radar. I felt safe enough to rebuild the reference of my life in my own mind — and so I kept going.

The year I got married, our first trip to Ocracoke Island, the trip to Costa Rica with Jordan, ooh, when Jordan was born, when I worked on the radio, and washed clothes for money, and the WIC lines, and the year the company started, and when we moved to Arkansas, the first time we went to Kauai.

I poured over journals to find where I'd betrayed myself or others. I was trying to remember who I was to create an identity to move forward—but it doesn't always work out that way. Sometimes you find a self that was more beautiful and kind than you thought. Or more loyal and tenacious than you realized.

I started to pour over 33 DVD's from a lifetime of VHS memories. Boxes of photos emerged to face who I was as a wife and mother. I braced. I knew how depressed, angry, bitter I felt. What would the photos show?

I didn't see what I feared. At all.

I saw a woman who was connected, kindhearted, laughing, and nearly always in the kitchen or giving a gift. I put these on the paper in blue marker… who I was at given points in time.

I noticed part of my past was traveling, writing in green marker under certain years the countries I'd been to, the beaches, the states visited. It all counted— no trip too short to chart.

Everything counted – from my first memory to the moment I held the blue marker.

Red marker scribbled writing and speaking, even sometimes media that played a role in my work — radio, TV, magazines. Suddenly I jumped to how I could force this as a career, how to jumpstart my life, the 5 strategies I could use – and everything locked back down. I was lost, with no forward movement.

So I walked Banjo, knowing that these were last days with him.

When I walked him, no neighbors asked me how I was earning my life. They just loved me. We talked dogs and laughed. I could just be.

In time, following patterns and passions on pieces of paper scattered on walls as maps of a previous world, I slowly came back online. I joined a group called Magic Making Circle by Hannah Marcotti and where I learned about holding life, being in the gray, and trusting women who were also watching their lives show up.

In the group nearly two weeks, I began to feel safe enough to post a few days a week. Determined to keep balance of living in the real world, I listened to my body, soul and mind.

Baby steps, but life was emerging.

Slowly, speaking engagement offers started. Interviews on podcasts began again. Social media for The Mom Whisperer ramped back up just a few days a week sharing other people's work, not creating anything new. I wasn't ready to fill my retreat yet, the one I booked earlier, but that was already reserved and waiting.

A very different person showed up on the other side of 10 weeks than the one that went in.

Dinners were slowly becoming a ritual of care.

Baths were no longer earned by "doing enough" during the day. Intuition started speaking matter-of-factly and very quietly.

I was starting to find my own life.

Because of these 10 weeks of falling apart and putting the puzzle pieces in my pockets, shifts that happened remain accessible treasures. I never did put all pieces together. Some I can't pick up, and others I still can't find.

Of course, there's more to healing, but honestly, I'm still not quite ready to look over the daily journals I kept over that time frame. As well, it's not time to dissect the subtleties of healing, although I'm sure they happened between the cuss words and the figuring out dinners. There's a curved line from there to where I am now, and for that, I'm indebted to Heather, my therapist, and those friends who kept showing up fearlessly.

"Sometimes it takes darkness and the sweet confinement of your aloneness to learn anything or anyone that does not bring you alive is too small for you." – David Whyte

David Whyte and Krista Tippett, The Conversational Nature of Reality, On Being, 4/6/2016. https://onbeing.org/programs/david-whyte-the-conversational-nature-of-reality/

From here, we'll go back to the FearLessFriday posts that continued.

CHAPTER #124

That Time When...

A few weeks ago, when I had a ton of time, I took a Saturday night and went through all 33 DVDs of the past 19 years. I don't know why I thought that was a good idea except that I grew up watching home movies. I literally had never seen these VCR tapes now DVDs and I had them since July.

They waited in the One Day basket.

I decided to be open to seeing whatever popped up.. cracks, things I missed, things I didn't want to see, how I was as a mom, family that passed away. They weren't in any order, so I never knew what was coming.

Of course things had a bigger context now than they did then. But in general, the thing that surprised me most was how much love was often around.

Several hours in, I saw a three and a half- year-old Jordan and me running around Battleground Park in Greensboro, NC. I was following him and he said, "Gonna get you!" but he wanted me to chase him. I forgot about that game where I'd tackle and tickle. We were laughing so hard.

And then he stopped, came to me, and took my hand and said, "Let's talk".

And plopped down on the ground.

And so did I (thank God).

And he babbled something, and waved his stick, and I said something about the clouds.

It lasted all of 45 seconds — on the ground, looking up, saying nothing and everything.

That was not a memory I held with me all these years. I have often credited Jordan with wanting to connect but maybe because of exhaustion, or distraction, never really understood our dynamic at its' best.

Of course, I started crying, and needed air and a break because the memories started to flood in. The park wasn't a rare moment- I savored connection with him.

I thought of the talks before bed, after reading a book.

And the ones in the morning at 4:30 am before I went to work.

And the ones at Toshi's coffee shop over chess games.

And during Survivor nights with chocolate chip cookies.

And about being bullied, and about girls, and about colleges.

We've been talking as long as he could talk, and maybe as long as he could listen.

Guilt is easier, and maybe more "humble".

But to look objectively, and let pop up that the essence of my motherhood was good, if not really good, that's a whole shift that we don't often make.

So I decided, at the end of 19 years, and nearly 5 hours of family movies, I'm giving myself my own verdict: I was a great mom.

Because I connected. And listened. And chased, and tickled, and let him be who he always was even as I bobbled to correct, and guide, and stabilize.

And loved hard.

Isn't it prideful to say I was a great mom?

Don't know. Don't really care.

Because who I was before I watched those DVDs was a pretty guilty, regretful, fearful mom.

But afterwards, I realized how much I had no idea that I was ROCKING it.

To this day, that young man is who he is — fun, creative, high integrity, independent, and deeply connected to me. There's no higher honor, compliment or marker of motherhood than allowing someone to be who they really are and maintaining connection.

Because he didn't have to. And I didn't have to.

And we did and still do.

There is one thing I would totally change if I did it all over again.

I'd believe every single day that I was enough.

And let that "enough" help me make the shifts and changes into more enough—ness.

Because love is always enough, and somewhere I forgot that.

And that night I remembered it and it's moving everything forward.

CHAPTER #125

Two Hours

So, when I was fairly convinced yesterday would be the worst ever, (because first Mother's Day alone) I took a bath and when I got out I realized I was in there for two hours. TWO hours. I think that means I've graduated to a new phase of motherhood.

#ANDICleaned

CHAPTER #126

One Day I Will Not Be Afraid

I visited Jordan in LA a few weeks ago. The apartment's Wi-Fi was weak so I needed somewhere with daily, reliable service.

I found a co-working space within a 10-minute walk. Co-working is a hub for entrepreneurs where they can work, meet, and network.

Except, to get there, I had to walk alone- in LA.

One of the things I'm working on is not being irrationally afraid of getting out/showing up. I know this makes no sense (because adventuring), but it's the truth.

I decide the next morning I'm going to go for it and walk. But then the inner rabbit trail starts:

And then someone will ask me for money, rob me, yell at me to go back to North Carolina, or try to get me in their car.

OR. *Someone at the co-working space will be mean to me, they'll placate me because it's "a nice mommy website", they'll charge me more because it's just a week, they'll all look like movie stars and I'll be afraid to say hi and go back to the apartment and hate myself for being insecure because they're just people.*

I didn't even leave the apartment and I shot the whole day.

My motto in a pinch has been, "Don't make sh*t up" which I learned from Diane, my acupuncturist who challenged me to stop living in my head.

It took me over two hours to start walking.

Fast forward a week — it became a walk I dearly looked forward to in the Santa Ana winds. Everyone at the office space *did* look like they belonged on-screen but they were super helpful and kind, and my hours were productive.

The last morning as I was walking, a man with a gym bag ran out from a parking lot in front of me about 50 feet. He turned to look at me, said "Oh shit!" and bent down, cradling the gym bag.

I kept walking because honestly, I had no clue what was going on.

But he kept looking at me and at the bag and I realized, "Oh shit. He stole that."

Nobody else was walking on that block. Cars were at red lights but not near me. There was no one to flag down and everything went to slow motion.

So I kept walking toward him. I don't know why. Yes, I do. I move toward danger. I don't run and it will be years of therapy to get rid of this.

As I kept coming (fully thinking I'd know what to do when I get there, but no words were coming to me), he stood up, slung the bag over his shoulder like it was his and swaggered back where he came from.

And I passed him.

And as I passed him, five credit cards fell out of the open zipper.

"Oh SHIT" and he bent down to clean it up.

To this day I'm not sure what I was supposed to do.

LA is big city. I know it happens all the time, but I'm not used to it and geez Louise it happens so fast.

I had no way of stopping or engaging, or even any inkling of what else to do but keep walking.

If it was my gym bag, I'd of wanted someone to say something.

Unless it was someone who didn't know self—defense.

Then I'd want them safe.

I was going to edit this because there's such a discrepancy between moving toward danger and yet doing nothing/ not knowing what to do/ no happy ending here.

But I'm going to leave it because sometimes things are still in process...

I still force myself to go out.

I know that means I may face unexpected things. I can almost count on it.

But showing up is always my win, even when I just don't know what else to do because the bigger regret is staying in.

CHAPTER #127

Letting Go But Not Yet

A few weeks ago, Banjo refused food. No ground beef, chicken, fish, nothing.

But I needed him to take anti-seizure medications if nothing else.

In a last ditch attempt before going to LA, I gave him leftover kielbasa from Easter with a few pills tucked in.

Pretty much, he has fully recovered.

Daily kielbasa "treats" are what he lives for.

Sometimes he looks at me and I know what he's saying, "Where's the beer? The cigar? Work with me here."

#WorldsMostInterestingDog

CHAPTER #128

Carrying Extra Weight

A few short months ago, I was waving and smiling at neighbors trying to be neighborly. I'd heard from more than one person that the last people who lived here included someone wearing an ankle bracelet on house arrest, and an "uncle" who imported a variety of girls from France. I kid you not.

One woman in her late 60's wasn't having my friendliness. So, over time, I just smiled until I finally ignored her because no sense in driving her and me crazy.

Then I was walking Banjo near the mailboxes and she made a beeline for me. She said, "He looks like a lion" (because his winter coat rings his neck in a mane formation), so we bantered back and forth.

Finally she said, "Four families here lost dogs to old age in the last 18 months. Mine had tumors and I finally knew it was time." She had tears in her eyes. It never occurred to me that having a dog would be a trigger for others. It wasn't about my waving at all.

She continued about how her husband now needs her, leaning for support because of his health. He has a cane. And her.

She reminisced about having kids, and dogs and letting go. It was a beautifully normal life.

"It sounds like you've carried a lot of weight for a long time."

She squinted, "What does that mean?"

WHY would I say that? I cannot get out of it. I totally offended her. So I stated the obvious with as much connection as she'd allow.

"Well, I just mean you're a really strong person to have carried your dog with tumors, and of course your kids before that in a lot of ways, and now your husband and his health issues. You've carried a lot through the years." And then I asked God to open the earth so I could be swallowed. Or at least find a way out. Just walk away, nothing more here.

I've learned that really strong women can't afford to crack.

She half way smiled, looking straight through me, "Sounds like people need to start carrying their own weight. I've been doing it for too long. I have my own weight to carry."

We laughed.

Every little bit is enough.

It's all really enough to just show up.

CHAPTER #129

Dig Deeper

Sometimes life is like a chicken pot pie — everyone only sees the top crust... but if you dig deep, there's a bottom one too.

CHAPTER #130

Things to Be Jealous Of

We don't really talk about jealousy, but I think it's the hidden thing that messes things up.

We see only a tiny slice of others' lives — rarely the big picture.

We almost never see their pain/ suffering.

We then see only the good through our own life lens — the thing we don't have, want, need is what we zero in on.

Ultimately, it isn't even about the person anymore, it's about us.

Been working on killing that for 10 years, so I get it.

Over the course of the past 3 years, people have told me they envy me for a variety of reasons (insert your favorite reason of choice here).

On the receiving end, I have felt small, ashamed, wanted to hide, wanted to give them whatever I had, explained why it's not that great, feared they would no longer want to be my friend, or downplayed it.

In short, my reaction was to disown the parts of me that made them uncomfortable.

So the choice is a small life — teeny tiny— where I keep others comfortable and not threatened so they like me. Or, Door #2, I live authentically and let the chips fall where they may.

Fortunately for me, I already tried Door #1 and I know exactly where that lands. Heh.

Door #2 has been a bit trickier.

The more I wholeheartedly commit to showing up full on, the more competition and jealousy pop up.

Classic true example I hear often: That I don't have to worry about making dinner for anyone anymore.

Um... because an entire season of life is complete and I'm eating alone every single meal?

Trade ya. I'll bring pizza and sit with the kids. Bet you wouldn't go three days without missing them.

So, if there's going to be jealousy, let it be over the things that really matter...

6 Things To Hate Me For

1) My clean junk drawer. We all have one but MINE is cleaned out every single month. BTW. It is as life transforming as you always wondered — effortless access to scissors, pens, info. It's the little things.

Value: $10,000

2) My relationship with Jordan. He doesn't live at home, pays his own bills, and is figuring out his life while texting me back "I love you".

Value: $19 Billion

3) Banjo. He is three years past dying because I've needed him. He eats kielbasa every day. He teaches me to sit on the grass and watch the clouds.

Value: $15 Billion

4) My parents. Both just this week sent me notes of love in some form. My step mom is best ever. There's no undercurrents or drama or unspokens with anyone.

Value: $47 Billion

5) My friends — who have helped me get the dog to ER, taken me to (just one) Air Supply concert, walked through art museums, had endless coffees, laughed, invited, pointed out, and known the mess I am. They are 25 years younger than me and up to 30 years older and everywhere in between.

Value: $25—30 Billion

6) My bucket list trip to Europe — that's worth hating me for. No defense on that one. Changed everything. Mainly because I got out of the room and didn't stay in it even though I asked myself every day "WHAT am I doing here?" ;—)

Money Value: Less than $5K. #StartSavingUp

If I'm to be envied, I hope it's for the love around me, the beauty of life, the things I couldn't buy that make my life valuable.

CHAPTER #131

You Will Know

It will be all right in the end, and maybe even in the middle. You will not suffer as long as you think you will.

You are not fated to be unhappy.

You are not destined for failure.

Remember who you are.

Let me say it again. Remember who you are.

Be gentle.

Practice exquisite acts of self-care.

You don't have to be as strong as you think you do.

You don't have to be wise and certain about your path.

Your frailty is beautiful, and your innocence too.

Getting lost is another exercise in navigation.

You can't fix everything you touch.

You won't break everything you touch.

Don't apologize if you're tired.

Don't second-guess your stomach.

Maintain eye contact with everything, especially yourself.

Fall to your knees at least once a day.

Say yes at least twice.

Love daringly, wholly, unapologetically.

Believe in magic.

Befriend your fear.

Look up.

Listen.
The birds will tell you everything you need to know about flight.
Forgive yourself your great sadness.
Unlock what hurts.
Make a prayer for loss.
Unpen your words.
Get messier than anyone thinks you should.
You'll know when you're ready.
I'll say it again.
You'll know when you're ready.
----Maya Stein, "You Will Know" https://www.mayastein.com/

CHAPTER #132

Bill Paxton

So. Bill Paxton (who passed away earlier this year) shows up in my dream. He's looking like Brock Lovitt, the sexy search ship captain in the beginning of Titanic, trying to find sunken treasure. His scruff beard, earring, and long hair are looking into a camera on a tripod on foggy Scottish moors.

No one else is around.

I walk over like we're old buds, "Hi! Looks like you're doing really well. So, can you tell me the secret of success?"

(Because apparently that's EXACTLY what every woman on the planet really wants to know from freaking Bill Paxton. Even in my dream I am inept with men. Beyond inept.)

He looks up from the camera, smiles, walks over to me and says,

"Yeah. It's forgiveness."

I felt my eyebrows go up into my forehead. One part, "That's it?". Two parts, "How?"

Seeing my disbelief, he takes the camera off the tripod and walks toward me, fixing the camera lens.

He stops in front of me, smiles and effortlessly offers, "Think about it. If you forgive, you aren't spending money on things you don't need to cover up anything, or pretend things are better than they are, or running away from something. Think about it."

Bill Paxton then turns and walks away to the tripod, puts the camera back on and disappears.

#JustThoughtIdShare

#MissYouBillPaxton

CHAPTER #133

We Matter Too

The month before Jordan was born, my husband at the time landed a sales job for a manufacturing company and we both transitioned from teaching high school to other worlds.

The company he worked for was run by Larry (not his real name).

Larry was one of the most amazing people I'd met up to that point. At 40ish, he had owned the company nearly 10 years, everyone loved him, he was incredibly successful, and personally trained his sales people.

But the one thing that always struck me was hearing about Larry's treatment of the 50 people "on the floor" who ran the machines and made it all happen.

They were to be highly valued, interacted with daily, given gifts at Christmas. Larry taught his sales team to understand they were never above the people on the floor because of paychecks, education level, etc.

The sales team knew names of their family members, gave all 50 people gifts at Christmas, knew who got their job back after rehab and hugged them.

The company thrived against bigger companies who were always trying to steal their people (as if any one person was the magic).

Larry had an amazing way with people, great family — kids going to college, beautiful house in a historic neighborhood, wife who loved him.

Then Larry decided to sell the company. He got a good offer, and could stay on helping with the transition.

Except on the day he signed over the company, the final paper was his resignation. They said, "Sign it or we fire you." So he did.

The new bosses didn't own the company, they were sent there.

Sales people left, or retired. Those who stayed were pushed for numbers and productivity. Many workers on the floor were let go or replaced so profit margins could be assured. Every year new bosses were sent in, more changes made, better profits demanded.

The company closed its doors a few years later.

So, what achievement matters? What was enough?

The cohesiveness of a company? "We are doing this."

The sale of one? "Hey, I sold a company."

The purchase of one? "Hey I bought a company."

Recognition, accolades, prestige, and honors are markers of recognition for excellence, jobs beyond well done, and TOTALLY are deserved at every point. This isn't case in point for underachieving.

It's case in point for achieving with heart, soul, values and family intact.

Ten years after signing his resignation, Larry walked into the woods and never came out.

His funeral was breathtakingly beautiful. So much love. So much loss. Standing room only of a 1500-seater. No doubt there were demons he alone was slaying and no one recognizes that kind of daily fight as an "accomplishment".

Clearly, I'm not in any position to talk about achievement. I recently had 15 minutes with a New York literary agent. I wanted to understand what it would take for my book, Momifesto, to be picked up by an agent/ traditional publisher. Everything was going well until he asked me if J. was in college. I talked gap year. He said, "But is. he. going.to. college." and I said "No."

And everything shifted. His concept of achievement and mine collided.

I had "nothing new" to offer them that I did "better than anyone else".

So what achievement matters?

Truth is, the one we say does.

That's my lesson these days: What do I say matters? Do that.

What's enough? What God and I decide — often on a need to know basis.

Knowing all I know about cultural expectations and norms, and hustling, and getting ahead... can I lay my head on the pillow at night and say I did everything I needed to do, followed every breadcrumb, and loved well?

#WeMatter

CHAPTER #134

Always Look for the Castle

When I was visiting Jordan, we went to his chess club at a cafe in Redondo Beach, California so I could watch him play. He won chess champ of his high-school so I thought this would be fun.

We arrived to a variety of men aged 20ish to 60, already playing or waiting for their turn. They were super kind to me and asked if I played, of course I said, "Not really."

Jordan says, "She taught me everything I know!"

I clarified that I taught him in 2nd grade and that was my level. That I hadn't played in a year. That there were so many reasons I'm not playing.

You don't walk into a chess club and think you're not going to play. So, a man who didn't have a partner asked me to play. He studied moves, ran fingers through his salt and pepper hair... and within 20 minutes, won.

Within five minutes he says, "Vikki, we have a request for you to play."

And I went over to the table and saw two men, early thirties, from Mumbai, India. From the tech industry.

The story was one gentleman was supposedly just learning to play since January and thought we'd pair up well. Because, let's face it, I'm a girl.

So we sat down and after exchanging pleasantries, realizing he's been practicing DAILY since January. I looked in his eyes and said, 'You are going to beat me. But you are going to work for it."

Because at this point, talking smack, as they say down South, is all I had.

He said, " I know I'm going to win. I just don't know how yet."

I'll admit. I wanted to crush him.

We were actually evenly matched.

So the game lasted a total of 90 minutes... which happens when you don't know what you're doing. Heh.

I keep telling him, "You'll win. But you're going to sweat it out."

Pretty much, chess is silent and normally you don't do this type of psyching out, but pretty much, I was desperate.

Around the 84 min mark, he had two queens because I forgot that if you get a pawn to the other side, you get another piece — and you always pick a queen.

So he says to me, "Ok. I'll give you the chance to ask my friend one question." He speaks to him in their language and the guy comes over and looks at the board and says, "What's the problem? You have a rook." (FYI: The rook is the castle looking piece, it can fly across the board straight shots only).

I said but so does he.

He said, but you have two.

And he sits down.

WTH? It made no sense.

So I'm all about secret messages and following the breadcrumbs in life... I look at my rook again and realize all I need is for him to make one fluff move of any sort, and my rook is sitting in a position to win. WTH.

He makes his fluff move.

I move my castle and humbly say "Check" although I know it's In Your FACE, CHECKMATE.

He looks and says, "What???" and hits his friend's arm. They speak again and the friend stands up, looks at the board and says "He had 2 QUEENS. What happened?"

I said, "You told me to look at the rook so I did."

He said, "But I didn't see THAT."

They both stood up, so I did too because I figured it was over. At home, loser cleans up the board, but I guess not in they're neighborhood. We shook hands, and they left saying he has to study harder and I cleaned up. I like to think the buddy was apologizing.

There's no gloating in chess. Wins last only as long as the next board. I was replaying the game in my head and what did I miss... and really, why did I think he would beat me?

But my bigger win was that I actually went.

And actually played. And talked smack, and laughed, and had fun. To just show up and see what happens.

So far, no one has ever yelled at me to go home, or asked me why I was there, or told me that I didn't belong.

That only happens in my head.

And those, apparently are lies.

Because I beat out a tech man (albeit a newbie) who had two queens in freaking chess.

Thank you for knowing me enough to know I would totally talk smack before going down but never ever if I thought I would win.

CHAPTER #135

The Thing About Creativity

Creativity requires the courage to let go of certainties.-- Erich Fromm

CHAPTER #136

Real Love Is

(Trigger warning: If you've recently lost a pet, this may be difficult to read.)

We told him goodbye a million times and it wasn't enough when it was time to let go.

We slowed the days down, and told him we were grateful for his love and protection of us. That we love him- and know he loves us.

We reminded ourselves of all he's been through with us— the moves, the storms, chasing rabbits and barking at deer.

I repeatedly asked him to promise me he'll visit us somehow in clouds or anything. In return he would always, always lick my face. Better than a pinky promise.

We watched him fall asleep, his face releasing more pain than I knew he bore.

And now we are in zero gravity, tired from crying, brains not thinking clearly, forcing ourselves to eat one meal.

Not forcing ourselves to eat ice cream.

We talk about loss, riding the waves of crying when we need to get it out. We talk about how it honors our dog that deserves all the tears we have.

I wanted to protect J. from this because I knew how hard it would be.

I wanted to save and heal Banjo.

Truth is, real love is doing the highest good for the other and still being there when it's what you wanted to avoid, when your heart is shattering.

Real love lets pain carve and chip away who we were.

And real love, I'm learning, is about letting go and trusting that God's specialty is holding all who free-fall, all who can't find due North, and all who are exactly where they most need to be.

I do not know who is supposed to take me for walks, and wake me up in the morning and finish this kielbasa.

But I do know love in a whole new way.

CHAPTER #137

Asking for Help

Me:

I'm going to need help putting my life together.

God:

Hold My beer.

CHAPTER #138

Aerial Yoga Because Why Not

I went to Aerial Restorative Yoga at Cirque du Vol in Raleigh, North Carolina with my good friend, Marianne, a roommate from college who invited me.

I talked myself into it with the logic that it's RESTORATIVE. There's wine and chocolate afterwards.

Besides all that, aerial silks have been on my bucket list since the winter. I assumed it would take years to pull it off, but the offer was the best ever because Marianne, who I adore, would be joining me.

There were about 10 women there——everyone's first time.

We watched the instructor just easily put the silks under her arms and sway back.

10 of us did it.

Then she leeeeeaned forward and the silks held her by the arms.

Done— ish.

Then she sits in it like a swing. This is not complicated, but you do have to pull yourself up into it.

Um... done.

Then she leans aallllll the way back, with her legs spread eagle, legs down and touches the floor.

She inverted.

She went UPSIDE DOWN.

Nobody did that for a full 60 seconds.

I've been practicing being mindful and listening to what's going on in my head.

It was very clear: *What the hell you don't INVERT on the 4th move... what kind of crap is this... I thought this was Restorative yoga and I'm going to die and never ever get that cup of wine and chocolate and now I have to make a moral decision to at least try this or hate myself and I hate you and everyone in here.*

Then I attempted it.

Because I will most likely never ever ever come here again.

And I did NOT let go but I did go waaay down and spread eagle (because if you leave your legs together, you go through the space between and fall). I held on for dear life.

Let me explain what happens when you death grip the silks while your body is slightly remembering being eight years old and playing on a swing set.

If you keep holding on, you rotate.

And it's not a rotate that you want, by the way.

It's a sloooowww, spread eagle rotate like you should start waving and people may start clapping and there is the slight sensation of vertigo that you're pretty sure will never go away.

By this point, Marianne was inverted as well. And from what I saw, holding on for dear life, but not rotating.

I said, "Hey Mar, stick out your arm so I can stop spinning."

Being the sole reason I was hanging upside down next to her, she did it, and reached out her hand, "Here". We would totally do anything for each other.

Marianne has a PhD in molecular biology. I have a Master's in Education. Neither of us specializes in physics. Because she would not have given me her arm if we did.

I grabbed her arm and as soon as I did, I changed directions and she started rotating. You see the problem?

I'm feeling that salad we had 90 min. earlier start to shift.

So. I'm spread eagle. Inverted. Holding on for dear life. And rotating. My roommate is rotating next to me. We are halfway laughing and halfway terrified.

I would like to say that if you told me four years ago that the culmination of the worst season of my life would end up here, I would have at least started drinking. At least.

I kick into survival mode and remember hearing earlier that if we're spinning we should touch the floor and stop ourselves.

So the choice is all mine.

Keep spinning, holding on and play it "safe".

Or Let. Go. And. Reach. For. The. Floor.

My mindful practice kicked in, *Holy Lord Jesus if You get me out of this I swear to God I'll let go of everything and anything the rest of my life if this is the lesson don't ever again make me learn this and please so help me God let the floor be right there or else I'm going to scream and throw up.*

And so I let go, bent backwards like I've never done since I wore keds and reached for the floor.

And the floor was right there.

And I stopped rotating.

And the teacher came over and said, "Now you can give each other a high five"

And although I said, "Oh, ok" out loud, inside it was all, *F*ck you F*ck this place F*ck high fives F*ck it all.*

And after I had no more f*cks left, I realized I'm ok.

I'm there. Not moving.

My head feels like it's going to explode. My legs hurt with the silks wrapped on them. The salad has continued to shift back into my stomach.

But I'm ok.

She tells us to come up and she shows us other moves and I do them.

More inverts. More leg bends. We do one-leg-in-the-silks-planks. I mean, once you invert, the rest is FUN.

Ultimately, we end up in cocoons, hanging from the ceiling with lavender eye pillows to block out any light, while she plays Desert Dwellers, which is like slow belly dance middle eastern music.

Marianne, who at this point, was on the floor, breathing, and trying to ease the seasickness, said we looked like we all had a rebirth coming out of our silks.

The teacher took a selfie with us.

We loved her.

We got wine. And chocolate.

Take what you will from this.

As for me, I found my f*cks.

Learned when to give them.

And learned when to let go.

#DoNotEverDoThisOnAFullStomach

#DoNotHaveAlchoholUntilAfter

#AlwaysSayYesToAerialYoga

CHAPTER #139

Life Needs Frosting

Counselor Heather: Our bodies will tell us what we need. I crave kale.

Me: Well, you're wearing green, so that works. I'm wearing pink. Not sure what that's about.

Counselor Heather: It's frosting.

Me: So busted.

CHAPTER #140

Kyrie

I am learning to navigate being alone.

There. I said it.

It's not a woe-is-me thing. Sometimes loneliness feels like hunger. Or a hole.

I accept that's going to be a factor— I just want to learn how to deal with it and not be so afraid of it that I run to the nearest 24 hour French bakery. I plead the 5th since I even know it exists.

I digress.

Really, I've worked it down to just a few hours of the day that are the toughest: Dinner and sunsets.

So! For a few months, I've rearranged things so my biggest meal of the day is lunch. Works on so many levels- its perfection. "Dinner" to me now is a protein bar and no dishes at 7 pm.

But the sunsets.

The past three weeks, I decided to lean in and drive into them or away from them. Just take my little protein bar and drive. It's nothing eventful. But it's glorious — fresh air, sometimes music, often clouds and light. I drive until it's dark then go home and it's better.

One night I headed toward Pilot Mountain. It's a straight shot out of the city. My playlist popped up Mister Mister's "Kyrie".

Kyrie elasion down the road that I must travel.

Kyrie elasion down the highway in the night...

(Perfection again, right? I put it on repeat.)

I realize I'm not going to get close to the mountain for the sunset so I take a country road exit and snag a field shot on the exit ramp just to get the colors. Three quick photos later, I'm finished. Back in the car, I drive toward a stoplight, and a million blackbirds land on the wire in front of me. It's so expansive, I can't even capture it all.

A full million.

So, I stop in the middle of the three lanes of the exit ramp and just take a few photos.

A black mustang pulls up next to me. I'm thinking either this is a cop, or someone is getting ready to yell at me — Hey Baby, or Get Your Prius off the Road, or Do You Need Help?

I roll my window down.

Probably, I should have driven off, but a) I wasn't done with the birds b)I'm so tired of running c)I'm not as afraid as I probably should be in these situations.

It's Mr. Handlebar Mustache. He looks at me and says, "Are you watching the birds?"

I said yes sir. Because it's Tobaccoville and "sir" is always a good idea.

"Man! You should've seen them earlier out near the valley! There were even MORE than this!" He's smiling, with no ill intent.

And we sit there for 25 seconds, blocking 2 of 3 lanes in the middle of the exit ramp, watching the birds, chatting about it.

Then he says, "Have a great night!" and takes off.

Maybe it's because I'm looking, or not looking, I don't know— either way it's not that hard to see that gifts are everywhere — specific, can't miss gifts that fly in, give a wink and fly away.

Loneliness is very real.

But when it's put in a back pocket and driven out to a sunset, it loosens its grip, stops yelling for French macaroons, and falls asleep before home.

I tend to leave it in the car.

CHAPTER #141

Just A Moment

Some moments to me sizzle... there's something electric about them. Like, a volt of Pay Attention.

Over the past few years, I've been collecting these volts... nuggets of experiences or truths that aren't satisfied with a photograph.

I need the audio.

The past year or so I've been randomly clicking on a few just to hear whatever I can hear now that I couldn't then... somehow using these pieces as much as photos to integrate life that's passing so fast.

So I have a collection of 124 snippets of audio that snagged me somehow. Nothing makes sense as a whole, except pushing "record", and the wisdom that only comes with being very present.

There are so many frozen moments in time that sound like they are happening right now....

The time I talked with my Uncle and he told me his life lessons.

The time I went to the entrepreneur's start up boot camp and had a marketer rip my book apart and then put it back together.

The morning church bells in Florence.

The street in Amsterdam.

The last conversation I had with Grammy about life, and marriage, and living your dreams.

Rehearsing the lines for the book trailer.

The conversation with Gram about forgiveness and letting go when she stayed with me for a month.

The blog post ideas.

Jordan and what he sounded like before he went to his dad's for the weekend or when we talked philosophy of art.

My very last one, 6/26/17 I began, "What if you trust yourself? What if that? What if you just trusted you were right?

I don't recognize my voice... it's deeper, calmer, with more depth. It's not the same one that I started with.

CHAPTER #142

Go to Hug Them

I am going to my high school reunion happening in a few weeks.

This should probably breed more fear in me than it does.

I don't even have a dress yet. I've finally enjoyed a summer not on a diet — peaches, corn, blueberries and I can prove it. My hair has yet to grow out from last year's cut.

Mom asked if I was renting a car.

"For what? Can't I use yours?"

Mom: "You'll be judged. People judge based on your car."

Me: "Is it the 98 Olds? If not, then we're good. There's no red carpet. Nobody is standing outside waiting to see what I drove. Most of us didn't even have cars a long time ago. Ma. I don't even LIVE there. WHO CARES? "

This is why I left at 17.

I couldn't navigate what I (fairly or not) perceived as a materialistic life, taking the train into New York City, where money was the consuming focus of my life. Working on Saturdays. Always in the shadow of people who lived in Greenwich or Southport and never "measuring up" because we didn't have as much as David Letterman or Martha Stewart. Pace of work that would barely keep up with the taxes.

Mom told me it was her 50th reunion this year.

She wasn't going because, "Why bother? There are only maybe 45 on the invitation list out of three classes. There used to be 612 of us just in my class alone."

"Oh my gosh, what happened?"

"The Vietnam War."

Last reunion, I was externally on the top of the world.

It was five years ago, I had a husband, a son going into high school, I ran a business. I had a dog. I lost weight. We were spending Christmas in Hawaii. My dress was spot on for the beach. The conversation in the car was warning him that men would greet me with a hug or handshake and kiss on the cheek.

But inside, I was afraid, insecure, maybe no one would say "Hi." Maybe they'd joke me for something stupid I said or did. Maybe x million maybes.

Except it didn't happen.

Instead, it was compliment after compliment. Remember when's that were so great, and funny. Impressions of my teenage self that I forgot and sorely needed to be reminded of. People who remembered me and loved me— not regardless or in spite of, but just loved me because I was one of them and they were there years ago.

Because of that night, my interior shifted. I believed them. Maybe that was the start of all things changing. I don't know. But four months later life as I knew it would start to unravel.

I would pull nearly daily on conversations from the reunion thinking to myself, "But they said... "

I was who they said I was —who they remembered me to be.

I am not coming to this reunion to hear one word about me.

I'll show up alone, and not have set answers to any question they ask. So, I'm hoping to make people feel really great about themselves if they're comparing (or have watched me drive up in my mom's car).

I am going because I'm set on returning the favor of hugs, and kind words, and remember whens and I-think-you're-amazing.

Someone may be facing things they don't want to talk about. Their own hell. Their own four months to it all changing.

Maybe it took all they had to even show up.

And I want them to hear me say that I remember them strong, and fun, and smart. Because that what will carry them — because they'll believe me— because I was there way back then, and here now.

#NDLegends

#GoToYourReunionsBecauseSomeoneMayNeedYou

CHAPTER #143

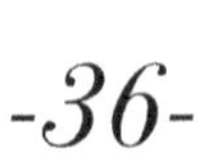

-36-

Sometimes, I remember to realize how beautiful life is.

Today's list:

1)The neighbor's dogs who no longer bark at me so we can finally talk and laugh.

2) Mr. Apples the tabby who appears randomly and belongs to everyone.

3) Finding a place that Finally will take me as a volunteer. Finally.

4) Licking batter bowls.

5) The gardenia that died earlier and came back to life this month.

6) The crepe myrtle petals stuck on my car

7) The messages of friends before CT

8) The soap in the bathroom AND the kitchen.

9) My family flung everywhere

10) Pieces of life that are really just mine.

11) Realizing I'm going to be ok (and that its ok if it took this long to have that moment of sheer belief)

12) Found 2 reunion outfit options today... maybe going with pants after all. It was effortless and I loathe clothes shopping. In fact, there's nothing I avoid more. So this was a huge one.

13) I'm loved.

I was going to stop here...not sure what's coming next... I don't feel like stopping yet...

14) The furniture I didn't get rid of and kept.

15) The mess that is my office because it inspires me

16) The continued lesson of Just Show Up

17) The Wi-Fi zone I passed through today that said "love"

18) The dog on TV commercial that looked like Banjo

19) Otis, my friend's dog on Instagram that looked like Banjo

20) Blackberries.

21) Today's commitment to get out of sweats

22) Ending today in sweats and the gym

23) NOT liking screens

24) Keeping Sunday Sabbath (even though it kills me and all I want to do is clean my desk and wash clothes)

25) Realizing for just this one moment, there are no impending losses that I know about and have to brace for and hold my breath for. Not. One. (that I know about)

26) Asked an artist friend to craft a tattoo for me and she said yes today

27) The checkout girl at Wal-Mart who was snarky to me and I didn't let it in.

28) Beyond gratitude for my body. Every wrinkle, and curve. It's a powerhouse. (I've been zero tolerance on negative self-talk and today was genuinely thankful in the DRESSING room.)

29) Kitchen is a mess and it means it was used and that feels like home.

30) Not saying yes to something even though someone asked. I said I needed to sit with it and they totally respected it.

31) I saw longhorn STEER today

32) I saw a HORSE today

33) I saw cornfields

34) I found two hawk feathers. I never found even one before!

35) I cried for joy because I felt I belonged.

36) The bathtub I'm getting ready to go in, regardless if it's 10pm, because it's ok. No one cares. ;-)

CHAPTER #144

Seeking Doris

Doris asks if there's anything she can do for me while I'm away. I ask her to look out for a painting I bought.

I didn't realize the guy was actually painting it, so I have no idea when it's coming.

Doris: What's it a painting of?

Me: A girl and umbrella in the woods.

Doris: I was hoping for a naked man.

Me: Doris.

Doris: Well just the back side.

CHAPTER #145

Be Right or Connect

(*Disclaimer: only my side... there's other viewpoints involved.)*

When I went to Los Angeles to visit Jordan who went there to do fashion photography, the Santa Ana winds were full on. It felt like a hurricane was 100 miles away but never came.

Jordan and I went for dinner and after he parked, I opened the door to a man in his late 20's in an army coat and high 70's style afro walking with a backpack who smiled so I smiled back.

Him: Great weather isn't it?

Me: Yeah but a little windy, don't you think?

Him: Yeah but it's awesome.

Him to J: Hey! She needs a hug.

J, taken off guard: What?

Him: She needs a hug. Make sure she gets one.

J: Ok. (man leaves) What did you say to him?

Me: Omg NOTHING he said something about the weather....

This happened about two days after I'd gotten there, and things between us started off great and turned sideways as things are prone to do when opinions are involved posing as facts.

Usually my opinions. My facts. Because, well, I'm right. ;-)

We'd been apart for 100 days, at my request so I could get my feet under me in an empty nest in a new tree. I expected to go visit him and see his world — his work, his home, his friends, his life. He'd been there seven months.

Only I didn't recognize his world.. or his routine, or how he did life. For example, he stays up until 2 am, driving around LA, goes to bed till 3 pm, gets up, does some photography, eats something around 5pm, hangs out with housemates. I didn't see a 9 to 5 routine, I knew he was applying to scoop ice cream and clothing stores, but nothing was popping. And he was sleeping until 3pm. And I started to question and freak out and talk about college and Plan B and every single thing any mother would do to have an opinion while she's freaking out inside and doing a bad job hiding it.

So we clashed.

For days on end.

And he hugged me and we kept clashing and regrouping.

To the point where I said let's take a day apart.

During that day, I went to the Japan section between LA and . the Santa Monica pier. Around sunset, I took an Uber to the beach and put my feet in the sand.

So, the next day we talk and I ask what he wants from me. I decided to default to connection — I gave up being right and East Coast swagger to just connecting. I would give him whatever he wanted as much as I could.

He spoke without anger, "I want my mom and for you to tell me what to do but not how to do it. I thought this was going to be different. You're just waiting on me for everything and I don't know how to run the days and you're mad."

I saw this person who is chasing their dream and yet barely old enough to drive... who is so far from home, but making their way... who literally has no experience at Chick-Fil-A but has done $1000 wedding shoots...

And he just needs me.

And I just finished 100 days trying to just not need him.

So here we were, in the middle of the Santa Ana's.

I'm sure I hid tears, but eeked out, "Jordan. I am always your mom. I'm here to cook a few dinners for you and see how you are. I'm here to tell you I'm actually really proud of you. But I will not disrespect you or your life to jump back in and run all this. I actually can't, I don't know this world at all. It's hard for me to watch you struggle, but I respect your process and however I can support you, I want to. I've not done that well."

We called a truce, and hugged.

Later that night, I hung out with Raynelle.

Raynelle is a friend from high school who has been out there for 20 years. She's from my hometown and embedded in west coast life.

But she's just my friend who happens to love Jordan.

After we hung out, she saw him.

"Joooordaaan!!!" hugging him hard.

She asked how he was, and very quickly he honestly said he didn't know what to do. He asked her for advice.

Long story short, she explained what he needed to do, how to do it and where. I am pretty sure she sprinkled fairy dust on him and said she believed in him.

Those five minutes cleared up his perspective and actions. They clarified his goal and next steps.

Raynelle was the fairy godmother he most needed.

The next day, he did what she said, I beat a guy at chess, and left for the East coast.

After I left, the winds finally stopped.

But Jordan kept going.

Following Raynelle's advice, he landed an internship at a top LA photography studio, beating out kids with resumes from colleges, and film schools.

On the side, he was a mover and drove a U-Haul through LA to pay the bills. He found a woman with an Etsy shop, who needed help with photos.

And Harper's Bazaar picked up one of his shots for their Instagram feed.

And he's doing a photo a day for 100 days.

When I left, I texted an apology for my part in how hard things were. That I loved him. He texted that it was all good as long as we got through it. We both agreed we did.

It helped me realize how resilient and forgiving he is. How much maybe we both needed to see that when you fight fair and hard and with love, you can get to the other side.

That assuming, and expectations, and being right

are poor avenues for connection or change, but they can always be undone. And layers of trust hold us both.

CHAPTER #146

How We Do It

I forgot that I'd not been home to Bridgeport, Connecticut for two years.

Although I was bracing to see a Noxzema cup in the bathroom and Aqua Net on my dresser, no such thing.

There's not even a phone hanging on the wall anymore so my friend Sue can call me.

Or boys.

I've been trying to get my bearings here, and I remembered that sitting in a coffee shop helps.

But Bridgeport, for all its new street signs and stores, hasn't changed...

We don't do coffee shops here. They are cultural and not needed here. We work — hard. We do. not. stop. for. coffee.

But we do stop for friends coming over to eat on weekends. And big laughter.

And if they don't at homes then they do in diners or restaurants.

I forgot about that.

It's either yes we can get together or no.

It's not a text the day before, "Hey are we still on??"

It's where all our ducks are in a row at all times.

It's a disparity of social class that would boggle minds.

It's races melting together while still being in hubs.

It's just an updated version of what my grandparents on both sides came to from other places.

Apart from my food bucket list, I've been spending time going through my Gram's things, helping my mom sort what to keep and what to give/ toss.

We're on hour 21... (7-8 hours a day for days.)

It's not like a rent bill for $18 from 1947 matters.

It's that it was a rent bill from a certain house, when my uncle was seven and got the family kicked out of the apartment for throwing a peach pit off the balcony.

We found the eviction notice and all it said was they wanted another family to move in.

Or that my grandfather's birth certificate says his parents were born in Austria....because politically, saying Slovakia, would mean something else. I'm still not sure. We aren't Austrian.

In my own journals, sometimes I write important things in the back so I always know where to look. Apparently, so did Gram. We found her stenographer size notebook that started in the back and she wrote a line every day my grandfather was in the hospital. Page after page.

Month after month.

And I remembered this isn't going to end well and she doesn't know it yet.

And five pages later it's just that he's hurting and can't eat.

No more entries.

Then the date a doctor bill was paid.

Life takes time.

The parts that matter most— happen in bits and pieces and those fragments are what's left when we're gone.

And I can't plow through them.

So, to get through the intensity, it takes friends popping in, and meeting me at a diner, and having us for dinner. It takes a high school reunion tomorrow that is long overdue to pull me back into life now while honoring the life I had here. It takes being reminded of Necco wafers, and boys, and my grandparents coming over to be there for us after school every single day to make dinner and eat with us.

And it takes time to go between worlds so that I can keep the strength and beauty of both.

Because I forgot how much strength and beauty there is here.

CHAPTER #147

Who Says You Can't Go Home

High School reunion was AMAZING.

I forgot how it is to just belong, unapologetically, no explanations needed except, "Where have you been?"

Where people just have a common background, and so much doesn't need to be said.

What does need to be said is, we have the youngest looking class in the history of all high schools ever.

The lines of "cool kids" and the rest of us are permanently erased.

I overheard apologies and forgiveness.

People reconnected and laughed and exchanged business cards.

No one asked about my car. Or my dating life. Or my job.

I thanked people for who they were back when… for the kindnesses, the lunch table stability, the time we…

I hugged and was hugged x million.

We will always have Canada. (Because after our class, no one else ever did. ;-))

Too many stories and Remember When's to post here, but halfway through the evening as I was laughing and exhausted, looking at the beautiful decorations, flowers, balloons and listening to Bon Jovi, I tried to remember WHY I left... and that it was okay that I did because apparently, I've been carrying so much of them with me, I just needed to remember.

Huge thanks to those who arranged the evening, invited everyone and made sure the food and alcohol were more than enough.

CHAPTER #148

Timing

So...I researched the eclipse because I live near—ish to Charleston, SC. But the traffic, etc.

I decided to just see whatever we got in North Carolina.

Not even buying glasses.

Then I booked a trip to go to Portland, Oregon (part work, part adventuring —and then I hibernate for the winter, I swear.)

A week later I realized the flight out there lands me at the airport at 10am. Eclipse totality is at 10:20am.

My counselor, Heather, has an extra pair of glasses.

Because, of course. It's what she's been doing all along - helping me see without going blind.

#BeyondGrateful

CHAPTER #149

Fear Factor

What would you do if you weren't afraid? ;-)

CHAPTER #150

Ms. Potato Head

A few days ago I asked "What would you do if you weren't afraid?"

It was one of my favorite comment strings ever.

Because so many wrote things that we all understand— a new life, job, saying the hard things, asking the questions that would blow it all up, and more. It's just an honor to be friends here.

So, I'll go.

If I wasn't afraid, I'd do online dating and speed dating.

Someone asked me how long it's been since divorce and I realized it's been three and a half years.

Omg. I immediately felt WHATS my problem? THREE YEARS?? Where have I BEEN???

But I remembered it's just that I've been Ms. Potato Head and my pieces kept falling off and I can't find the holes to stick it all back on and more fall off.

So I've just sat and let it.

Its ok to just be Ms. Potato Head for a bit, I know this now.

In time, new things have popped up...

It's been reconfiguring to interact with good men (*new eyes to pop on).*

I've needed my own work, adventures, hobbies, and interests so I'm not showing up as someone's mom with a iPhone of family memories on a first date (*new potato head outfits to pop on).*

I needed to calm down my inner sirens so everything isn't a red flag (*new hearts to try out*).

And its' taken time to dig around and see which pieces not only stick but that I also like. Because we all know just because the pieces go on doesn't mean they should. (*Hello side eyes*)

And sometimes you just need to rearrange them and get a new perspective.

And I wanted to make sure the eyes, eyebrows and the 10 hairpieces, three noses, and ears are all in the box before I meet people who try to tell me my pieces don't fit/ aren't right/ need rearranging.

And that my box of pieces is mine...and I can always share or pack it up. It's always my choice.

But it's still scary, even with all these shiny new pieces.

And ONE day I'll let you know how it goes.

But not today. And not tomorrow either.

#IThinkIveGotASpareEyebrowIfYouNeedIt

CHAPTER #151

Not Getting Lost

That time after a day of hiking in Oregon, I got into the Uber version of Cash Cab, while classical symphony music was blasting. He was a retired Navy Petty Officer who tracked the sun four times a day for 14 years.

He knows the time of day at all times.

If I were a party of four of more and the drive was 30 minutes or more, he had questions ready and I could've won an iTunes gift card.

After I get in he says, "Well! Didn't you order the party Uber ride?? There's Solarcaine in the back if you need it."

Sometimes I'm slayed at how lost I feel and yet find people who can always find their way and share it with me.

#JustShowUp

CHAPTER #152

I Spy

I spy with my little eye the good of ....

—the flowers that are hanging on for a little longer.

— the joy of 70-degree days

— they saved the lodge at Multnomah Falls

— the veggie pizza for dinner while I wash clothes, and feel this normal is beyond perfect

— the things I said No to today

— the messages that feel like hugs — that I'm giving them, now.

— that manchego cheese counts as a "hard" cheese

— realizing when I'm trying to gun my life forward and knowing enough to pull back because it's already in motion ;)

— engaging in politics behind the scenes

— trusting my feet a little more

— the friends in OR/ WA that I saw

— Women Who Run With the Wolves — for the 3rd time.

— That life is no more in a free-fall... and it's time to decide that Thursdays are the day I wash clothes again.

— my commitment to allow crisis to wash through and over me helps me process the changes the world is enduring without checking the news every 5 minutes (this is a big one)

— the friends in CT that I miss

— apologizing to my body for assuming it's just here for me instead of realizing its asking for things I can give

— trusting that the good that comes, is really mine ;-)

CHAPTER #153

The Truth About Waterfalls

I chase waterfalls.

Recently, on my trip to Oregon, I visited Multnomah Falls' dizzying heights, breathtaking greenery, unforgiving power.

I sat next to a woman who was six months pregnant and on her babymoon (last vacation before baby). She asked why I was there... I said because my son has been gone a year in LA, and I'm celebrating life moving on. And we smiled at the circle of life between us.

A park ranger guided me to a short hiking trail that very few people go on to find Wahkeenah Falls.

Again, so breathtaking that I spent a few minutes there.

It reminded me why I need waterfalls.

I cannot stop a waterfall.

My strength is no match for it.

I can't see where it originates.

I never see where the water ends up.

If I tried to stop it, I would drown, there is no point.

I went near it to cup water to drink and literally lost my breath — ice cold, and air like a force field of movement.

I didn't want to run away, so I did all I could do — accept it.

I let it be forceful. And cold. And powerful.

I'm still here, and nothing about it has changed, but I'm not trying to stand against it.

I can find my breath.

And for a minute, I felt like I breathed with the falls...

When life is bigger than I am, and my strength is no match for it, and I lose my balance and breath, I remember Wahkeenah Falls and all the falls before her that taught me to find my footing, and breath.

When I let it be whatever it is without changing or forcing it to be different, and surrender to it, I absolutely find myself.

And hear my next steps.

Sometimes it's to stay, or go, or help, or pray, or connect, or a million other things that come to me.

It's never "do nothing."

It always starts with surrender. And a little bit of chasing what I really wanted all along.

Wahkeenah = Yakima Native American for "Most Beautiful"

CHAPTER #154

It's Always About The Path

I visited a Japanese garden in Portland, OR and took a guided tour so I didn't miss anything.

What looked like a quick walkthrough to most became a profound exercise in perceiving.

We stood at a trellis when we began. I thought it was beautiful on its own. But the guide asked us to look at it again...

"Notice the last of the wisteria overhead. Step back so you can see how this is the frame for the next scene we're walking into. Look down. These are ballast rocks from ships that ported here in the 1800's. Whenever you see the path under you change, it means to slow down, stay alert, a change is coming, the scenery is changing."

We learned quickly to take in every scene like a sip of miso soup. Looking not only ahead but stopping to peek behind us, , around us and raise eyes up. Every nook, plant, height and collection of trees expertly curated with peace, beauty, stillness, and noticing a moment. The intent is that the observer is so carried away and considers their life that the gardens disappear and act just as a guide.

Notice.

Slow down.

Step back and look.

Look down.

Slow down.

Stay alert.

Watch for change.

Look behind.

Look up.

Always look up.

I've been working on doing this but in the garden it made so much more sense... because if I just take a minute to take it all in, I'm lead to the next thing.

CHAPTER #155

9 Minutes and 100 Years

When I was in Portland, Shannon invited me last minute to a concert by Five For Fighting. I knew who they were... the DANG 100 years song.

"Want to go?"

"I just Googled them. It's the 100 Years Song. I can't. I'm going to cry."

"Me too. Free ticket. "

So, we were good.

I get an Uber and a woman around my age is driving. We talk about the concert and how she's new to Portland.

She's from Portland Ct.Something in me wonders what's up with that because, well, Portland. *(From here, I need to change some facts so she stays anonymous.)*

She goes on to say she left everything on the east coast to pursue her dream life with her new online boyfriend who lives out here.

I look at the map on her iPhone. I have 9 minutes with her.

I take a few seconds to figure out my thoughts because DEAR GOD I need stop lights, and traffic and more than 9 min. and PLEASE DON'T ASK ME WHAT I DO (the whole mom whisperer thing is NOT for now). She's heard every bit of judgment already but I don't know what else to say. Of COURSE she knows this is wrong…omg don't say anything and just listen.

Her two kids visited a few months ago.

So I asked , "And then what?"

"Now, I drive and live with my boyfriend."

I lean in. Every red flag is waving, but I decide to go with it.

"Sounds like your soul mate." (not an ounce of sarcasm, I swear I dug deep)

"Weeellll, not really." She told me of cracks, and then asked what I do.

"Admin stuff" (which is technically true some days)

"You only live once. If that floats your boat." (omg.)

Long story short, two minutes to the theater and she tells me she wanted out for a very long time.

She felt her kids were old enough to understand— they're nearly adults anyway- 12 and 15. One out of the house at 20.

She was dying inside.

I understood.

Nearly every woman I know understands some tiny piece of this.

Nobody I know actually does it, though.

She must have really been hurting.

It's only when I was hurting that I wanted to blow everything up. I already judged myself six ways to Sunday, tried everything, and had to save pieces of myself that were left and maybe that's where she was too.

Maybe she didn't blow it all up.

Maybe she was walking from the battlefield.

We get to the theater and I see my friend.

"Here we are."

"Hey, just so you know. Sometimes our whole lives need to fall apart before we figure out who we are and what we want. I just wanted you to know it's ok if that happens."

I thought maybe she was realizing it already did. And was. And is.

I just wanted her to keep going and find her way out.

100 Years to Live by John Ondrasik
Performed by Five for Fighting
https://www.youtube.com/watch?v=tR-qQcNT_fY
I'm ninety nine for a moment
Dying for just another moment
And I'm just dreaming
Counting the ways to where you are
Fifteen there's still time for you
Twenty-two I feel her too
Thirty three you're on your way
Every day's a new day
Fifteen there's still time for you
Time to buy and time to choose
Hey fifteen, there's never a wish better than this
When you only got hundred years to live
#9MinutesIsAllSomeoneNeeds
#NotEven100Years
#YesICriedAndSoDidShannon

CHAPTER #156

Love What Is

Sometime a year ago, in the throes of selling the house, watching junk trucks come and guys take stuff to haul away, burying St. Joseph, getting a contract on the house, saying goodbye to Jordan... I had to decide where I was going to live. I won't say "alone" because it's so dramatic, but alone.

So after feeling guilty, I decided in my new world, if I could choose anything, I wanted water nearby. It was deeply intuitive and made no logical sense, even to where I should go. I spent 6 years in the woods, but I could never see the sky, so water was the wish.

There was a Saturday I drove near a lake and went up and down every street that bordered it until I found a man walking a dog who told me to check this one street.

So I did.

Long story short, I found a place with a short walk to water. And sky. I put a bid in to rent it, convinced it was due to grief and loss and I was making a really bad wasteful decision (I'd say selfish but well, there was no one else to consider, so.. whatever.)

I moved in sometime in November.

The neighbors told me about the former tenants and the "formal Japanese garden" that was there at one time.

I didn't care. I had water nearby.

Besides, it was just random bamboo that was growing and I had to keep killing, and rocks were missing anyway so no big deal.

Then, fast forward 10 months and I ended up making another deeply intuitive if not "really bad wasteful selfish decision" and went to Portland.

To the Japanese Gardens.

And after 2 hours in this respite and retreat, I realized: I HAD A JAPANESE GARDEN IN MY BACKYARD.

The bamboo.

The rocks.

The water—ish, nearby.

The path that changes its form when it's asking you to stop, wait, there's a change ahead, slow down, be here.

I went home.

I've been sitting on my rocks ever since. Apologizing for not getting it. For killing what was growing because I didn't know.

I asked my neighbor to tell me what was here — 12 foot tall bamboo that took her 3 years to remove because it encroached her property. The bushes that were different levels, now sheared uniform.

My stomach sank.

This tiny back area was stunning at one time.

But without understanding, care, and work, it was seen as a nuisance.

My losses, seen as a nuisance.

My life, without understanding. I hadn't even known where to start caring for it, so I've tried to make it as uniform as everyone else's around me... get the mail, do work, go to bed at 9...

But the shoots keep popping up (to do the retreat, to blog again, keep adventuring even on weekends)

And I am following.

Seeing what pops up.

What I'm led to and where and how. And no more thinking anything is wasteful, bad, or selfish.

Maybe the things we most need are what we have and just need to be shown what it is so we can love it even harder.

CHAPTER #157

Things I'm Made Of

The Before Bed List

Of the friends who spent time with me the past few weekends

Of the pile of logs I got from my dad and step mom and aunt for the campfires at the women's retreat

Of the mornings I slept in and reset

Of the rain that cooled things off

Of the leaves thinking about changing

Of the vegetable soup in the pot

Of the money to buy the veggies

Of the grace to not enter conversations that weren't openhearted

Of the quick soul truth of when to give my time and when it's wasted

Of holding my tongue and watching miracles

Of letting others be who they are

Of prayers that never go ignored

Of accepting a tattoo is inevitable

Of believing everything had to happen as it did for now to be the gift it is.

CHAPTER #158

Well, Good Morning

I struggled deeply with being afraid in Portland, Oregon. In spite of their incredibly low crime rate, fear locked me down. Eventually, I had to take baby steps to walk just down the street and back. Ultimately, I decided to stop being abjectly afraid of getting on the metro. Powell's four story "city of books" bookstore was my reward. I asked my host where the metro stop was, googled what exit to get off, and finally just did it.

I got on and realized I had no idea where to get off. The stop I was looking for didn't exist on this route. I fought panic.

A train worker got on the next stop and sat near me. I said, "Excuse me. I'm visiting from out of town and don't know what stop is for Powell's. Can you help me?"

He looks at me and smiles and says, "Well good morning to you. Look at you. You came all this way and got on this train and you made it! Here you are!"

We talked Red Sox vs. Yankees, and west coast life instead of east coast life. He told me exactly where to get off and how to find Powell's.

This was one of the defining moments of the year.

When I move past fear, life is just one foot on the other side.

Every. Single. Time.

I know enough life strategies, psychology and spirituality to fill 10 talks. But give me one day where I am so lost on what to do next, trying to get out of my own way and my own survival mode and Boom! Serendipity happens. Some call it a miracle. Some just coincidence. But one moment of that is worth more than all the books I could read.

Not because I made it happen, but because in the middle of it, I can finally hang in there with fear and see the beauty waiting on the other side.

Especially when it's a city of books waiting for me.

CHAPTER #159

A Kind Note to Amazing Men

I had lunch today with my amazing friend, A Man Named Kim, who asked me, "What can I do?" about the #MeToo posts.

He can't post #MeToo even in solidarity.

Yet he sees the immensity of women after women posting -his friends and relatives- and he wants to step in.

I thought of all the good men, kind men who have advocated for me in a million ways. Maybe they too are seeing all these posts, wanting to step in the ring, but unsure of how without overstepping or mis-stepping.

So, I want to offer initial thoughts I've had. These are imperfect and based on my own experiences, and no doubt fall short or maybe even misguided. But they are some practical starting points for amazing men to look for.

1) Work is like a second home. Please stop joining in, even to save face. I get you can't take on the boss or your male co-workers right now. But can you just look down and not join in? I don't want you on the outs and made fun of — it does no one any good. Just consider how you might not *add* to the culture. I think this may start to extinguish it.

2) If you see a co-worker fending off a man, please ask her " Is this a welcome conversation?" And from there, please consider your options. I am always humbled at how men deal with men. Your presence speaks volumes to other men. We see that all the time.

3) Double check home. Are sons allowed to pick on the daughters for "being girls" or weak or whatever? Is derogatory talk about girls at school allowed? Would you step into that?

4) In your personal life, are you clearly working on looking into a woman's eyes (instead of her chest) when talking to you? Stopping any porn addiction? Considering women as equals even in your own thoughts? It all trickles out and we feel it — we have to, it's our survival mechanism from any potential danger even if you intend no actual harm.

I don't seek to overthrow men, or call for power plays against you. I can't express how grateful I am for your steadfastness, concern, advocacy, and cheering women on. Personally, for all the men who are my friends and brothers — grateful beyond words for who you are in the world.

But if you want to not be silent, and help start a little change, these are some ways that are meaningful to shifting a culture into safety, value, respect and love. If you want to be part of a shift, I totally believe the opportunity will pop up. It's okay if it takes three to four pops before you say something (takes me more than that sometimes to be brave).

Gratefully, Vikki

CHAPTER #160

Restore

My friends texted this week asking how the retreat was in the Outer Banks that I led last weekend.

I needed a week to sort my brain and figure out where to land.

And I landed in this one moment, on the second night when we were at the beach and made a small fire at sunset.

It started to smolder out.

I had a second of panic and then realized — I made last night's fire, I made this one, I may have to start over, but I can make this one again.

So, I built a tiny starter patch under one of the logs— paper, fat stick (sap) my step mom gave me, and kindling. And it lit.

I thought, "I wonder why I didn't panic" and I realized — because I spent nearly two years building fires in a fireplace on weekends with nothing else to do. In a split second I thought,

"What else have I been learning?"

It hit me... the 20 years taking a weekend away alone to sort myself, using Birthday and Christmas gift money to just go and breathe and rest...

The past four years I've learned to listen, deeply, and with open heartedness, in a variety of situations.

The past year, I've had to learn to implicitly trust that what/ who is in me already is greater than any tip, book or training.

All of the past experiences, no matter how "tiny" or "pointless" they felt, were combined into a weekend for amazing women.

It's why I knew we needed sleeping in, time for listening and activity, solitude and fire, water, and air.

Because there's nothing wrong with us.

We just need to hear and remember what's already there.

And when we met it was new moon, made for wishes.

One morning there was a field of shooting stars just before sunrise.

A working hot tub on the back deck.

And in 48 hours, women quieted and smiled and laughed and knew again whatever they forgot... because more than learning, they spoke, and told their stories, and at night, we listened to the waves, while the wind blew away the untruths, and the fire burned away the limitations, and we believed again that everything is possible.

Tonight, I end the moderating for the retreat FB group and from what I've been watching this week — they are doing exactly what they are made for in the lives they have.

It's been nothing short of humbling to be part of.

CHAPTER #161

The Scar

I have decided there's not an answer to fear. There's just responses.

I'm pretty sure I'll always be afraid of failure, success, letting go, doing the wrong thing, doing the right thing for the wrong reasons, etc. etc.

Convinced.

But I'm also convinced of this amazing truth:

That I can have the response of : So what if it does?

So what?

If I fail, succeed, let go, do the wrong thing (again)— so what?

Then I'll face it.

And learn.

I mean, what if I live alone and burn myself and also end up with chiggers that made bruises on my arm AND tendonitis in my shoulder — then what?

And what if it was during a time where I was trying to heal my life and just wanted to force a few decisions and push a few things forward

Then what happens?

Then I may end up in the urgent care, where a doctor might have to deliver a message I probably need to hear:

"This is a second degree burn. Most people don't realize that healing takes much longer than we wish it would. And often it leaves a scar."

What. The. Heck.

So what?

So what if everything in life had to slow back down to a crawl, a few friends needed to come by and help me out, and I decided to nap, and read books and dream some more, because clearly you can't hurry healing. Of anything.

All you can do is create the conditions for it to heal itself.

The speed of healing, the outcome, or the scar — not up to me.

Learned that one.

Healing for me is always 1 part surrender, 1 part naps, 1 part Just Do The Next Right Thing and two parts implicit trust that I'm where I need to be. And if I'm not, a complete stranger will let me know.

So, I may always be afraid of something.

But my new supreme spiritual lesson, well, since the spring, has been, So What?

Thank you for reading. And for knowing I am and I'm not as crazy as these make me sound. □

#IBurnedMyArmRoastingVeggiesInTheOven

#ItAllHurt

#YepTheresAScar

#SoWhat ;-)

CHAPTER #162

Six Ways To Sunday

Thank you.

To the Facebook people who share that they had surgery and how it's changed them.

To those who are in loss or grief, or funerals and then opening Xmas gifts.

To the moms and dads who are bragging about their kids.

To the silence breakers and edge pushers changing the game.

To the tree huggers and nature lovers who embody protection.

To the country lovers who honor history to remember and not repeat it.

To the open minded and hearted who are not dedicated to any cause except what they know is right and good for all.

To the crypto coiners who are ushering in new paradigms.

To the adventurers and entrepreneurs who are discovering their new worlds.

To the God lovers and angel believers and Jesus huggers who let love shape them.

To the spiritually connected who say the craziest things that are absolutely true.

To the worn out women who are funny, and brave, and keep showing up for their families and lives even when they don't have all the answers.

To the men who embody amazing fathers, husbands, boyfriends.

To you when you post something and then question if you even should have because you cracked your heart open six ways to Sunday.

You inspire me.

Keep Going.

CHAPTER #163

The Tip

I went solo to a restaurant the other week. Brand new journal, old IPhone, pen cluttering the table when the waiter gets there so I don't look as solo as I am.

I order an appetizer and main course tell him this is a judgment free night because I'm not going to eat everything.

Somewhere in the middle of asking how the spinach dip was, the waiter asked what I do.

I waited tables and I know this is odd.

So I tell him a vague admin answer.

He says, "Don't take this the wrong way, but I just thought you were an author of a book."

I shake my head and laugh. I tell him I'm busted and I do have a website and book. He tells me "no judgment" about my vague first answer.

When he clears the appetizer I ask him what he does (because no waiter's goal is lifelong waiting tables).

"I manage the restaurant across town and wait tables here. I've only been here 60 days, moved from Miami." He's smiling without a care in the world.

Except, I remember 60 days ago Florida was hit with a hurricane and I ask him about it.

"I lost everything. People feel sorry for me but look at all this, I've gained my life."

Through the course of the meal, he suggests I eat the orchid on my salad— or at least try it.

He tells me he used to be in sales and had everything and lost his soul.

So he went on a "Buddha walk" and sold it all, ended up in Miami in construction.

Ended up fleeing and making goodbye videos during the hurricane as he was evacuating.

"As long as you're breathing, you have hope even if you lose it all."

I order dessert, not in the mood for chocolate, I end up with Key lime pie.

The meal ends, I try one tiny orchid petal and he's right, tastes like cabbage. I tip a little extra and leave.

I drive away thinking he was probably shamming me that I'm naive and glad at least I didn't tip him more than I was willing to lose. He was probably lying the whole time just to get a tip.

The next day I go to pay my credit card and see a pending charge — my meal. Without the tip.

Maybe it's ok to let people be whatever version of themselves they most need to be. It always comes down to actions over words.

And the last thing anyone needs is judgment — on what they eat or how they survived anything.

Maybe just accept people and let the rest sift itself out.

Lesson learned.

CHAPTER #164

The Middles

This photo is from February from the middle of a covered bridge. I needed this whole year to understand why I took it.

I went adventuring and found a covered bridge off my path. I took a lot of photos, and saw the symbolism... maybe this is the light at the end of the tunnel?

Except it wasn't yet.

This day was a middle — a photo with light from both ends. My first adventure out after holing up for two months, realizing the gravity of the 12th loss in three years.

I could walk either end out of the lit bridge, but in life, there was only one way to forward.

And this photo reminds me how the whole year was a middle.

My body aching with grief waking up day after day in an unfamiliar place to live, the routine that isn't one, the new counselor, and wise friends.

The refusal for dinners which were the hub of a family I didn't have, and yet the commitment to let the new surface, even if it was just a day at a time.

We don't give time to loss. I think we fear being swallowed by it. And I was.

And then I wasn't.

Because there are middles.

And a new way to do life from desire, and wishing, and curiosity and attempts — all with no agenda for how it turns out.

I failed forward like a 4 year old boy on ice.

And I fell into family and friends, and life surfaced as I was told over and over it would.

And the year that was a middle is now my favorite year of my entire life. So far.

I don't say goodbye to this year with anything but gratitude. I bless it for carrying, carving, and creating foundations for all the new ahead.

Because you can't stay in the middle forever.

It just feels like it.

Until you look back and realize the middle is actually 10 months away because every day was one day forward.

Thank you for being part of the middle and the after middle, and the aheads. For reading and commenting and joining in.

May we all be there for each other's middles and new beginnings.

And even the endings.

CHAPTER #165

The Thing About Joy

I have been wrestling with joy.

Halfway, thinking "so what? Who cares? What do you do with it?" because it should have a purpose, right? □

Last week my favorite poet, Maya Stein, offered to give a motto for the New Year. So I asked for one.

She comments back, "My North Star is Joy."

WTHeck.

She didn't get the memo that I was over joy. It was too great a burden. At least there was a scientific path to happiness — joy not so much.

And although there was a little joy bubble that I could neither deny nor extinguish, I had no clue what to DO with it.

Surely not try to lock into it as a freaken North Star. It made no sense.

This is poetic, but not utilitarian.

Days later I randomly opened Brene Brown's Braving the Wilderness to page 144:

"The foundation of courage is vulnerability — the ability to navigate uncertainty, risk, and emotional exposure.

It takes courage to open ourselves up to joy.

In fact... I believe joy is probably the most vulnerable emotion we experience.

We're afraid if we allow ourselves to feel it, we'll get blindsided by disaster or disappointment. That's why in moments of real joy, many of us dress rehearse tragedy... I call it foreboding joy.

The only way to combat foreboding joy is gratitude.

Across the years, the men and women who could most fully lean in to joy were those who practiced gratitude. In those vulnerable moments of individual or collective joy, we need to practice gratitude."

Gratitude, joy, courage, vulnerability.. the simmer pot of life, turned on high with a few cinnamon sticks and orange slices added in.

Maybe joy asks to show up, hopeful, trusting and seeing what happens next. Because regardless of how it's "useful" it really does matter.

CHAPTER #166

And a Fire pit

I decided to do just what I could toward that dream of a mom ranch. I've had lots of input and warnings and business advice on how it's a waste to be in one place when I could go to the different coasts.

So last October I led a women's retreat — just in case it wasn't my thing I could bail on the whole ranch idea.

Maybe it's too crazy. Maybe no one will come and there's my answer.

Except it was my thing.

And they came.

So I went home and after a few weeks of Do I or Don't I— I decided to do it again, and booked another place, this time on the beach.

The real estate company called me 2 months later— they needed my house, could they upgrade me at no additional cost?

I said I didn't want to sacrifice quality, and I had to have beachfront.

So they sent me the link to my new place...

To 9 vs. 7 bedrooms.

To a brand new 2017 parade of homes house.

And I'm like Who's leading a retreat THERE?!?!?! I thought this wasn't my thing? I was just thinking a few nights away and now this?

Ummmm.. so... now this.

I've decided the only thing scarier than listening to a dream is acting on it.

The only thing scarier than that is when it starts to happen.

And every point fear never leaves. I realize deeply its just there, and to thank it, assess all the risks it shouts, kiss it on its forehead and keep going.

Because fear is a worthy companion but poor guide.

Trust offers clarity.

So does joy.

And if I can suspend fear of failure for a skinny minute, I might look around and enjoy the scenery...

And I have no clue what the retreat theme will be but I hope someone will be there because otherwise, I'll be sleeping in a different bed each night.

CHAPTER #167

Notes to Self

The 10 (ok 16) things I always forget...

1) I am not alone. Ever, never, ever. Unless, the bathroom.

2) I am guided by Love. Forever and always. STOP freaking out.

3) Laughter heals in places I forget need healing.

4) Goodbyes are part of the deal. They have to be.

5) Middles are essential. For 1000 reasons.

6) My heart is 10000 times wiser than my head. And my head is pretty wise. Always always do the math.

7) I no longer care who other people say who God is. He speaks for Himself. He's got me.

8) People are sh!tholes — not countries. You can tell them by their actions. Always. Bar none.

9) Generosity, Kindness, and Joy mess with people's heads more than anything else. Be it anyway.

10) I'm not made for small. I've tried. Really really hard. It doesn't work out for me.

11) Failures don't define my worth. BTW. The Lessons from those learnings expand me.

12) Maybe I'm the only one who wonders if I can pull my life off. Stop it. Like yesterday.

13) Its ok to not give a f.. Just, the things I do give a f. about, give a really big f..

14) I may never have a word for the year again. I need paragraphs. Or, at least a phrase.

15) The only thing worse than "failing" is doing nothing. Because then it IS a fail. Refer to #1—13 and keep going.

16) All I have and all I am is already more than enough. Everything else is frosting on a cupcake with fudge in the middle. With sprinkles.

#NotesToSelf

#KeepGoing

#Sorry About The Grammar I Know Some Had Really Short Non Sentences But I Had To

CHAPTER #168

Grammy

When I was nine years old, my parents divorced.

I don't remember when my dad and Leslie took us to meet Grammy and Daddy Joe, her parents, but I remember what I thought.

That I'd be really quiet and really good so they'll like me.

When life is upside down, and you don't know what to expect, it's easier to be very small and hide.

Except, you don't hide at Grammy's.

They were from North Carolina, my first taste of southern hospitality. For decades, every visit meant being met with absolute delight that I was there, some kind of food (or pie), and inevitably, other kids around playing upstairs or at the lake— swimming, waterskiing, ice skating. No need to hide, unless others were also hiding and someone was finding. The only reason anyone was allowed to go missing was because they were curled up with a book in the back room. Every wall was covered with books and no one was to be disturbed if they lost themselves until dinner.

Every time I left, I'd look straight up at a sky with more stars than I'd ever seen. The air somehow thinner and crisper than in my city just 45 minutes away.

Thanksgivings and Christmases were always at least twenty people laughing and eating and watching football. Their home was the gathering place— complete with stockings hung by a real fire. Daddy Joe would add logs every once in a while. Every Christmas I'd leave with more gifts than I could hold.

Through the years I'd call her and she would tell me stories of anything and everything.

We'd end the same way every time, "Vikki. I just love you." "I just love you too Grammy."

I visited her before she moved to a nursing home. She could no longer go upstairs to the room where 20 gathered and there was no more fire in the fireplace but I was to find something I wanted and take it.

I found three small Christmas books.

My stepsister ,Mary, offered to take me to visit her this summer. She was in and out of lucidity at 99. But she knew each of us, and asked about family and friends from the past.

Grammy: "Are you writing your next book yet?"

Me: "Grammy, I don't know what to write about."

Grammy: "Write about me, of course!"

Of course.

I visited her for one final time this past weekend. A quick blitz to CT as the twenty family and friends gathered at the cemetery for a final "love you", complete with roses, food afterward and lots of hugs, more than I could hold.

And always stars... but now one more to look for.

They don't make 'em like that generation any more. May we carry on their best grit and grace.

Updated: Grammy, you were right. There was another book, and you really are in it.

CHAPTER #169

When Fear Wins

I made a decision for myself that involved making a change— so there was loss involved.

I assumed that since I initiated it, I could totally handle the anxiety that would happen (as it often does with change because seriously, I still do love control and the familiar).

I felt a little twinge of fear and ninja blocked it with, "Can you believe how, in this moment, there is peace and you are ok and everything is enough?"

No lie. It was. It is.

Then my brain did a side kick into abject fear and anxiety: Holy freaking crap what did you do—what were you thinking—and now what if someone hacks your email or there's a food shortage or you'll never have enough to retire and then what— you'll live with your mom for the rest of your life. YOU did this.

YOU should have known better.

Funny. I hadn't even moved an inch and yet my whole reality shifted.

So I asked my FB friends what do you when there's this kind of fear? And they answered. Their answers are below— because I'm betting I'm not the only one and sometimes knowing you're surrounded by really smart people who care is 1/2 the help you need, so I'm sharing my amazing friends' answers.

I started to practice all these things. I was in the mode of all of it when the reality of Valentines came and I realized I'm alone again. And the reality of a shooting no one saw coming that stole lives. And the reality of a world in need and I want to help and don't know where to start other than fly to FL but then what?

So I kept the fearless practices in place.

Because then I can keep showing up and answers come...

I had a great talk over lunch with a friend.

I returned calls and had conversations with women who were doing really well after rough times.

I made vegetable soup and biscuits for dinner.

I mean, what if I stayed locked up in fear and didn't even return the calls, go to lunch or make biscuits? The consistent practices help me listen to truth vs. fear.

Here are the things I'm working on, from my friends who are really smart, and kind:

1) Box breathing — 7 seconds inhale, hold for 7 seconds, exhale for 7 seconds, hold for 7 seconds. Repeat. It's a Navy Seal trick and Erica, Eileen, Patricia, and Kellie reminded me to just do it even though it's sooo simple. ;—)

2) Happy Distraction— songs, movies, anything to shift the focus just a bit. Anything from Bob Marley "Don't Worry About a Thing" to Mosaic's "Tremble" to What About Bob—— all favorites of Hannah, Diana, and Erica.

3) Being present, facing it. Feeling it all and letting it wash over and you come out on the other side. Truth is, if you don't loop and look for more fear, it most likely will let go. (Doing this also brings me to the moment, and gee whiz, look all that's NOT actually happening right now.) Thanks Monty Winters.

4) Gratitude. Because always. Thanks, Eileen, Shelley, Patricia.

5) Remember the last time something fearful happened and how I overcame it. Remember the strength and overcoming and how I can use those same skills again. That's a little gem from Sweta.

6) Prayer. Because sometimes you forget that you're not God, you're not the one who caused something, and you don't have to figure

it all out on your own. And I needed to be reminded by Dorothy, Jenny, Susan and Hannah.

7) Just do the next thing. Get up. What needs doing? The dishes? Dinner? Vacuuming? A shower? Do. That. Dorothy said to. ;—)

Truth is, I'm very very good at dealing with things. Sometimes when there really isn't a crisis, my brain is like " NOW WHAT do I DO???" and those 7 things are what it's doing now.

We're all in this together... may we all find air and love and hope when we need it most. Thank you for reading, today.

#DontMakeSchtuffUp

#PracticeBeingFearLess—ish

CHAPTER #170

Brownies and Martinis

I recently saw Dylan and Bekah, trying to squeeze in time before their wedding in 55 days (or so). They are technically Jordan's friends but somewhere we adopted each other as family. Just because.

I didn't need a son. Dylan didn't need a mom. But apparently over time, it just is.

During my recent visit, the three of us went to the art museum, and then they initiated me into the world of virtual reality. Probably, I should not have gotten into a car in this world within 10 minutes of being in another. A different world felt layered on reality and this was both familiar and disorienting.

Over a brownie and martini at Chili's, I asked Dylan how we even came to know him and how did this all come to be?

He told his version- a parkour jam in Washington DC and he was taking film and somehow met Jordan. They hung out and since then, just are.

But as he recounted, I remembered the background.

He came in the middle of a family splitting.

I remember talks with him about how Jordan is younger than he is and do not lead him down any paths that I have to go down to find him. I remember my questions for him and who he is that turned into honest stories.

How he used to explain he was a coffeetarian and loved the fact that I had a coffee bar set up.

And how he never flinched when he stayed with Jordan at two homes instead of one.

He'd been there already in his own life.

Dylan was one of the most singularly stabilizing factors in a world where reality was layered on another world. His easy smile, and willingness to eat chicken pot pie for the millionth time, his thoughtful answers to any questions I asked, and always asking what can he do to help me — soul gold.

He and Bekah are both photographers...I have photos of me and Jordan thanks to Bekah I'd never have otherwise. Selfies only go so far.

I thought he and Bekah would disappear as soon as Jordan went to CA. The empty nest collateral damage is the loss of your kid's friends coming over, eating pot pie, playing video games and jumping on trampolines. I didn't contact them, giving them the choice to not "have to" visit.

But Dylan and Bekah were both at the log cabin that day when the coffee bar was gone and the trampoline was taken down.

He just looked at me and got it.

I think when people are fearless to ask to be in the mix when life is being stacked into boxes, those are the ones you know have their own stories of great loss or suffering.

They don't expect life to be different than it is.

They wanted to come and be in the shift, so they can say goodbye to that season for them as well.

And because they know you are still you. And maybe need a hug— or a photo. If you ever look through my Facebook photos, the ones with me and Jordan outside on stairs, smiling, light behind us, and Dylan with us, those were the ones Bekah took. The day the coffee bar was gone-and we were all saying goodbye to a house but not each other.

The gift to me, to this day, is their willingness to keep coming over, or still hanging out and just catching up. And always always taking pictures even when we were one less. Gratefully, they never gave up their passion or talent for photography. Dylan is now a high-end videographer at www.DylanWadeFilm.com. Bekah just started teaching, but her gift is photography at www.BekahMortonPhotography.com. The back photo of me for this book is her talent. Together, they are a force of connection and kindness, art and love in the world. They are my people.

I don't know why people choose each other. Maybe when no one has to? Maybe when there's kindness and laughter? Maybe because you're needed as is?

We don't have any guarantees in parenting, no five steps to brownies and martini's. But over the years I have learned that connection matters. Not only doing the work to connect, but letting others in as well.

Apparently, I've had some really great teachers. ;-)

CHAPTER #171

Invited

Truth is, I've been having to face fears of all kinds to make a decision to move forward with my dream of doing retreats. I still questioned this even though after I rented a place for a retreat this October they gave me a free upgrade to a 10-bedroom luxury home versus a 7-bedroom luxury home. So, of course, with the dream of being surrounded by sunsets and sand with others, I settle this, and decide yes, I'm just in.

Then this week a podcast invite. And a few days later, my friend, who happens to be an award-winning author Penny Williams asks if I'll be a guest on her upcoming Parenting ADHD Summit. Later, she emails if I'll speak at Happy Mama Retreat for moms loving their familes and facing special needs. *https://if-mama-aint-happy.com/*

I'm trying to wrap my head around not blogging for almost two years and there's still the green light to do this with invitations as signs.

Just show up. Really? Just be all in?

And I've been in re-brand mode because I'm not who I was two years ago... and yet maybe even that's as it's supposed to be. Maybe there are new perspectives that are needed now. Guess I'll find out.

I had it all together and now it's all together in a whole different way.

So, here's what I've been working on.

New everything— even the retreat page is there.

I've learned a ton from the last retreat, (hello we need BEACHFRONT) and now this one is leveled up. And then leveled up again because they upgraded.

Because the world is leveled up.

And we need time, and air and ocean to find due north in a world where we've been put on the high heat cycle and left to dry.

Regardless of my brand, this retreat is specifically not just for moms but for all women at all stages.

I would love for you to consider coming even if you're afraid all you'll do is cry or sleep the whole time (maybe especially if that).

Life isn't what I thought.

I thought you build it all up, the 5-20 year vision, the slogging it out and then you retire with a margarita. Heh.

I didn't expect that you build it up, and some things fall away and some things stick.

And some things find you and won't let go even when you don't hold on. And the margarita can happen, but you don't wait for retirement to share one.

And that showing up is part of life, not just "on the way to life". I'm getting it.

CHAPTER #172

Pho

Recently, I spent a little time at the NC coast—68 degrees, empty beaches, free parking. It's my favorite time to go— my once a year solitude retreat where I listen and plan and dream. It's the once a year rhythm most familiar to me for decades now. I stay in a chain hotel, 15 minutes from the beach. I know where the best diner is, and the Trader Joe's for granola bars, and shampoo I forgot to bring.

Often, I'm sleeping and writing, holing up in ways only introverts understand.

But I required myself to leave the room twice a day. Once for sunrises and slow walks before the wind wakes up. Two, for lunch — anywhere, just eat. Dinners are always granola bars.

Inadvertently, I stumbled on a used bookstore (I swear, I just passed by) and across the street was a Pho cafe for lunch. Pho is Vietnamese comfort soup that pretty much reminds you to add Vietnam to your bucket list. True pho takes about 10 minutes to get to your table, hot, with a side plate of mint, cilantro and beansprouts.

You don't just eat Pho.

You savor Pho.

You realize you're in no hurry with Pho, and let it do its work on taste buds far too used to granola bars.

I sat at one of only eight tables and it was 11:50am.

By 12:05, the line was nearly out the door, every table filled, including the bar stools that lined the window. It was my first time there so I had no idea how popular (or amazing) this was.

A woman in her seventies in line with her husband began glaring at me. My *Graveyard of the Atlantic*, freshly salvaged, kept me engrossed with shipwrecks so I stopped looking up.

She and her husband eventually asked to sit with a silver haired Asian couple, but then for some reason came to my table to ask to sit.

Of course.

"We'll just sit here and not bother you."

"You're not bothering me at all..." I moved my book, and the napkin holder. "I just didn't want to sit at the window."

"Well, then people glare at you. Like me. "

"I know, it's ok. People sit with each other all the time in Europe, so this is no big deal."

She told me about her trips to Europe.

And how this Pho cafe came to be.

And how they had a place at Kure beach, 45 minutes away, but they were in town to go to the doctor. I didn't ask. Sometimes people just want to be more than their diagnosis.

When their food came, she told him how to eat, how not to eat and use a napkin.

While he had an easy smile and no slurred speech, I was betting a stroke.

I finally realized she was afraid.

Maybe of losing him. Maybe of being embarrassed if he spilled his soup. Maybe of not having a seat and having nowhere to eat.

I didn't ask any questions- about work, kids, or their names.

Maybe they could just be here, as is, without a story, and eat.

Maybe their biggest problem could be if they need more mint or more beansprouts.

I never know what to expect when people enter my orbit.

I never know what people need.

But I promised myself last year that I don't automatically "meet needs", because usually, I'm in error, and it drains me.

So all I can do is be there.

And I'm learning that ends up meeting more real needs than I would ever meet otherwise. There's nothing to fix. Nothing to prove.

Score one for Love.

CHAPTER #173

Coming Home

A while ago, Jordan had two internships and freelance work in Los Angeles. One of the freelance jobs, a premier photography studio offered him an entry level job. He accepted.

Then I got a call: I can't do this. I need to come home.

I asked him to take a few days to think this through. We talked. There was a moment where I thought to myself, "I'm talking him into staying. I've lost my mind."

There were many factors involved in his request.

But the one I can tell is he just needed to be closer than 2000 miles away.

As he drove home, I was getting my place sorted for him, but I was angry.

I've been grieving, trying to find my own inner compass of North again, pushing myself to move forward, figuring out life if the only factor to anything was "What do I want?".

My life was just starting to really be my own, after decades. I just wanted to walk around without a bra, talk to myself and sometimes fart. I didn't want to explain the whole bottle of wine when I only have one glass and dump the rest. I was done being momagamous, focusing my entire being on him. I wanted to keep the momentum of life that felt so deliberately built, beautiful and my very own.

At some point after he came home, I wrapped my head around the fact that he's not just visiting. We had "the talk".

"I don't have a TV and I'm not getting one. I'm going to date. I don't cook dinners anymore, you're on your own. Your curfew is 12:00."

"Can I have 1:00?"

"Yes."

As we negotiated everything, I knew we'd fall into a routine at some point, but for a while things were bobbling. After our 3rd round of me pushing him to go work out, go walk — it wasn't working.

I realized he was ***in grief.***

He didn't come home to a log cabin, or dog. His friends were in college, or in LA, or moved. And an entire life he built on the west coast didn't work here. We don't have actors and singers and photography studios. That life was gone too.

I realized he didn't have due north.

He didn't have a compass.

So we backed up. We went into grief/ finding life mode.

I knew that world.

That world isn't sparkly. It's tears, and sleep, and inertia, and trying, and driving for no reason meeting teachers or Dylan and Bekah for no reason until you start to land somewhere. It's invisibly real and no one can go there with or for you, but your soul always knows the way if you listen instead of think.

Long story short, he's in community college with a view of life that most of his classmates don't have yet. He's impossibly smarter than I ever remember him. We are transitioning into a more equal way of being in the house.

And instead of him imposing on my life, he's adding to it in dimensions I never expected. Mostly, this new family requires me to hold onto all the places I've come to be— independent, having preferences, and in bed by 9:30pm.

There's always room in the house for us both, even for me.

CHAPTER #174

How to Grow Hair

Two years ago I went to Los Angeles with Jordan so he could prove he could get a job and a place to live, which he did quickly.

So, I splurged and went to a famous salon — no clue what I was thinking. I just wanted some occasional curls. Thought this salon could help. At the least just a blow-dry. At worst a full head of extensions. I was desperate for something. At that point, no matter what I did I couldn't grow my hair. Here's what I've been learning after two years...

How to Grow Hair (and maybe a life)

1. I had to second guess my current hair's possibility... is this really all there is? My whole life I was told by hairstylists my hair is fine, limp, mousy and they don't really like working with it. It kept me near them, because omg who ELSE would put up with this? An LA stylist would. Sometimes listening to other's opinions keeps us close to them for all the wrong reasons. I've learned those with no agenda are often supportive, smart, and know how to handle whatever mess you think you have.

2. I'd have to understand it. As he pulled straight up, he explained there's nothing wrong with it. Its biggest problem was that it had been straight ironed, highlighted, and blow-dried to a crisp. It's enduring what it wasn't meant for, so it keeps breaking. Sometimes we have to realize what's breaking and find out why instead of blaming.

4. I would have to sacrifice what little I had. It would take 3 years to have what I wanted. He said it with compassion because he knew I didn't want this. He told me he had just come out of a relationship and intentionally cut 12" of his own curly long hair. He knows it takes

three years to get it back. He understood completely— nothing heals quickly. Nothing.

5. I would also have to agree to a completely new way of life —no straightening. No highlighting. Yes to color. We didn't even know what was possible, so it needed time. At this point, I couldn't backtrack. I couldn't agree to getting out of the chair and going back to straight hair—I'd ultimately lose what I had. So although we started with two, I let him cut off four inches. Because once you see the way forward, you have no reason to stay where you are.

6. I learned to trust the process. Every day for nearly two years now, I've flipped my head over wet, and let the curls do whatever they wanted. No demands. No guarantees. Believe the curls know what to do without my help. Yes to biotin, manganese and windows rolled down in the summer. Believing that patience with the process will move to the outcome— even when there's very little control over it.

7. I learned who to listen to. Once I went home, I had to guard against the well meaning stylists who offered highlights; ignore their perspective that this was problem hair. I didn't go back to stylists who always cut shorter than I asked and didn't hear me. Ultimately, I've been on a quest for other stylists that would team with me now that I had a long term plan. I've been shocked to find (many) super helpful people along the way— which only bolsters courage to say "No" to those not in my corner.

8. I don't like middles very much. But at some point, people would start to say "I love your hair," and I started to realize it was growing. Really growing. Maybe you don't even realize when you move out of a middle.

9. What I wanted was completely possible. I have the curly hair I had no clue was possible. It's the hair I envied on others. It's what I went into the salon to get. And although I still have another year to goal (can you even imagine???), it's finally worth everything it took to get here. Everything amazing takes time, space and a smidge of trust and support.

I can't replace my LA stylist, but a local stylist one town over is where I'm settling. Brazilian by birth, but European by trade, I didn't have to apologize, or explain. He didn't offer me highlights. Maybe I wasn't ready for him a year ago, who knows? But he is my hair's soul mate.

Forcing, bending, playing small makes things like curls, souls, and hearts, break. But belief that there's more, wow. That's where the axis of everything shifts, isn't it? There finally is a light at the end of a tunnel and it's more than I knew to hope for.

I always think hair is petty, and yet, it's really about so much more.

CHAPTER #175

Weird

People are weird. Me included.

#AndBeautiful #AndQuirky #Unpredictable #Faultless AND #SupposedtoBeHereAsIs #MeIncluded

CHAPTER #176

Pour Me Another

I'm a Jesus girl, but not like I was, or how people think I should be. I'm sure I disappoint some because I don't talk Jesus or Bible verses, or Resurrection Day versus Easter in my posts. I don't demand "Merry Christmas" or prayer in school.

I'm okay with that.

I live in the Bible belt, so what I'll write may be odd or foreign if you don't live here, and completely rebellious if you do.

I know the God that requires things — obedience, Bible verses, evangelism, bringing up a kid with morals, submission to a man in marriage, and then take your pick on pre—Tribulation, mid—Trib, post—Trib.

If I do this, in return, I get family, friends, a 50 year anniversary celebration, grandbabies, and a retirement plan. It's a perfect codependent, manipulative agreement on all sides.

Except grief and loss shatter everything, especially false gods.

Because those are seasons of life where I couldn't keep up with all the "shoulds" while trying to process what was happening. So I let God off the hook of all the shoulds too.

So I no longer demand and hold Him to every "promise" in the Bible, wagging my finger at Him, telling Him how things are supposed to be done because "YOU said you would."

I no longer blame myself for not enough faith and that's why life blew up. Nor do I do it to others because seriously, we're all in process; **especially** the people who think they have it all together (Christian or not).

When it's Easter, I borrow other people's church services.

I need either air and sky or I need soaring cathedrals. Last year I was alone. So I needed anonymity and no one with good intentions saying, "How are you doing? We should get together". Outdoor service by the lake, slip in and out, unnoticed, go home and I think I made lunch for Dad and Leslie. It's such a blur because first Easter without Jordan or screens was just trying to get through to 9pm and jammies.

This year, Jordan with me, soaring cathedral was the medicine.

We know no one. It's perfect.

We shake hands with people around us and the Woman in Pink smiles, has it all together, husband next to her, looks me dead in the eye and says, "I have four grown kids. This is the first time I have no one home for Easter." She turns back around.

What the heck just happened here? Wait a minute.

I'm immediately in tears and the sermon didn't even start yet.

God isn't really supposed to show up HERE. It's a SERVICE and we're supposed to show up for HIM, and be sinners, asking for forgiveness again. We're not supposed to show OUR suffering (today is EASTER). We tell others to trust Jesus and go home to lunch.

She broke every rule there is.

At the end of the service, I broke the rules.

Because this is the life I've come to realize is "normal" for me. If God doesn't have any rules about this, and she doesn't, then game on.

I reached out my hand to shake hers and stepped in front of her. "My son wasn't home last year for Easter. I felt disoriented and lost. I'm so sorry your kids aren't here, I get it."

She kept smiling and said, "Oh, it's okay, we'll go to lunch.... But next year I'm not doing this. I'm going to see them or they will be here." I told her I know. And it will be different.

I hugged her, then stepped back to get my coat and told her she can go (we were holding up the aisle). That's the rule.

"I can't. I'm so disoriented. I don't know where I'm going." There are cracks, as reality sets in about her day ahead.

"Then take a minute. It's ok. I understand."

And she did, her husband standing patiently next to her.

Jordan and I left, and I assume so did they.

I have no grand ideas of who I think God is anymore. Father/Son/Holy Spirit (*fyi – the last one is feminine, look it up*) has blown my mind — both in allowing so much loss, and in showing up in profound ways to heal, help, and enjoy me. Pretty much, my spirituality is a tall glass of showing up, some cubes of lessons, a twist of breaking some "rules" along the way, a rim of trying to see how we're all so connected, and a long generous 12 ounces of trying to default to Love -the kind that is courageous and transformative. One tall glass of Dayyyyum that He pours every day.

CHAPTER #177

Pancakes Two Rows Back

A few weeks ago, I was in a pancake diner with Jordan and Dylan. In walks a man who was vaguely familiar with a woman I didn't know. I asked Jordan, he said it was a dad of a friend he knew when he was little.

I looked back at him. Them.

My mind flashed to place him exactly with the family he was no longer with. Remembering them, I knew the wife was at church with the kids while he's here after an all-nighter with her. They looked rough. Like, overslept after a long night drinking kind of rough.

I realized how easy it is to date when kids aren't involved. When it's just wild weekends and scrambled eggs for breakfast from the diner and no dishes to clean up.

It's the easy way out.

Of course she's not nagging, and not asking for anything, she probably has her own job and didn't stay home with his kids, trying to balance a budget of food or clothes or sports. It's easy.

The way that is so hard is the day in and out. The sleepless nights because someone is up sick again. The years after year of watching kids grow. The choosing to change and celebrate your partner changing because life demands it.

Sure. She was pretty. Her smoker's voice. Older than him. No wedding rings.

And now she was his life.

And all I wanted to do is message his ex and fumble and say something...

I didn't know. I'm so sorry. I know you're at church with the kids. But he did you a favor. Or maybe you did you the favor. I bet you're asking yourself what you did and if he could have stayed and I just wanted to say, No. No he could not have. Because you deserved more. Maybe he was already gone and you didn't realize because life is so much. I don't know what happened but let me tell you this — your load is lighter, your life is unraveling but it's also unfolding, and you are learning to fly even when it's not easy. It's not fair. But at least your life is yours. And from two rows back over pancakes, it looks like you're the lucky one.

CHAPTER #178

Vision Drive

In my new life, ;-) apparently nothing happens in a straight line.

I move forward often by gratefully responding to things that cross my path. This podcast, that interview, this new course that needs design and proofreading.

And then, inevitably, there are the moments or days where I slow down, get scared, or sad (read "depressed", "confused"). I totally forget my vision, and what I was trying to do and why. It can look like inertia, but I've learned there's always more going on.

Waiting and listening can be mistaken for inertia.

So, I promised myself to always always listen to myself in those times. To lean in. Often in coffee shops like I was taught on a plane heading to Amsterdam. Or on long drives to nowhere as long as I love the road.

I can't push life in a straight line like I used to (and which I was very good at). But to keep showing up, especially when I can't see where all the dots connect— maybe that's where real life happens. Go get a coffee. Go drive. Read something.

So, I did.

My head was in a thousand directions at once, but then there were fields and cows and hawks...enough of them to erase the incessant "what if's" and "omgs", and "now whats".

I drove 60mph on a blissfully semi-empty two lane highway that's straight but forks several times. Finally, I was settling into the sunset and thought, "Huh. So when do I turn around?" because, knowing me, I would drive for a really long time.

Then this sign popped up for the next exit: Vision Drive.

Not only was it a marker for turning around the car, but turning around the thoughts.

I've hated the question, "What do you want?"

It means nothing after profound loss. It feels futile. Last year I spent months asking if what I want even matters if a) I truly may not get it so enter in shame, guilt and failure and b) it can be taken away so why bother.

So, vision and I have had to wrestle a little.

Actually, we've wrestled a lot, because in my self— help world, everyone talks about vision and where you're going and on and on. How it's the best way to get anywhere and how it's the only path to your perfect life. I've spent weeks helping clients define their vision. Geez. It's nearly sacrilege to NOT be mentally tough, make a plan, push through to the goal until you score.

But my body and mind have pushed through and cannot sustain that driving force.

So, Vision and I have come to a working truce... now, it's what's bubbling in my heart. It's an invitation to hear it again, get clear again, remember where gravity pulls me.

It's an offer to feel and believe —even if just in my imagination. Because there it's real, and it matters and it counts.

So all the pressure for it to show up a certain way, and in a certain time frame is off. It doesn't mean I don't try or set a few deadlines.

It means I don't demand promises that Vision never offered. It means I don't do straight lines, only segments— while keeping my eyes open. And that's really the only vision I need.

Truth is, nature doesn't do perfectly straight lines either. Maybe it's because the things built on curves, like a nautilus shell, are really some of the most structurally sound ever created.

And every swirl of coffee shops or long drives, isn't just going in circles, it's a new level of strength.

CHAPTER #179

Healing Crooked

When I was in college and grad school, I volunteered once a week at a homeless shelter prayer breakfast.

At one point, I had a fractured finger splinted from a brief but glorious run in intramural basketball.

One of the men— dark skin with a dimpled smile and an army jacket— noticed my finger and asked about it.

A few weeks later when the splint was off he asked again how it was and how far could I bend it. I showed him the extent.

"What you really need is a tennis ball. You have to use your finger——squeezing a tennis ball will bring the muscles back stronger."

"But its sore and I'm afraid to re-injure it," I confessed.

"But the bone is set now. The rest is to get back to using it. That's what we did in 'Nam. The last thing you want is to heal crooked. Get a tennis ball or something and use it."

Almost at every point in my life since then, whenever things have gone a little sideways and I'm finally out of the crisis, I'm always watching out for the crooked places.

The unforgiveness, bitterness, being afraid to be seen, being afraid of others, and/ or putting meaning on the situation that isn't true——I caused it, I deserved it, I should have known.

Those are some crooked places to heal.

They bend life into a half used place without full range of motion and not only hold me back, but allow me to settle for a new normal that isn't necessary. It's been after the fact that I've realized it.. when I'm frustrated, pushing hard as if it all depends on me, or making decisions out of fear. All could be new normals — but they don't have to be. I've learned that there are options to using other muscles.

The tennis balls for me have been getting back into the world, creating, doing, trying, bumping into mistakes and being grateful anyway. Forgiving again. Calling fear out and moving forward anyway in trust.

Sometimes it's a little hard because the context is a completely different life.

But it's one that's not healing crooked. Nor breaking.

CHAPTER #180

Serendipity and Restore

I had recently split our family finances down the razor's edge middle. The first act of physical separation.

The first check I ever wrote from my own checking account was to a retreat called "Serendipity".

They emailed me a welcome to which I replied that I will be crying the entire time. They said they would be glad to have me.

I knew no one.

I'd always gone for a weekend away by myself but that year I couldn't be alone — even if I didn't know anyone else.

What I didn't realize was that I needed anonymity, and women, and silence, and new perspectives.

I needed to hear other women talk about their lives. And divorces.

I needed classes that asked me to create art, learn vision booking, and learn to feel my body again. Where everything felt frivolous and pointless beyond hanging it up on the refridgerator and yet promised me answers I couldn't otherwise find. I met tons of new friends, who to this day, are still connected.

There are photos that exist of me actually laughing. Ironically, the ones on my website, are from this weekend.

I know that retreats have changed the trajectory of my life.

I've learned that three nights away is the magic number for regrouping. We never get three nights to just be.

So, I'm inviting you to my retreat in October called Restore.

I want you to come even if you're going to cry the whole time. Even if you don't know anyone else. Even if you don't know why you want to come.

Even if you're the one who "can't" go because they'll "fall apart without you". Especially if that's you.

I hear so many times how exhausted and overwhelmed women are, and I know for sure it doesn't have to be that way. When we take time away and sort, we find answers that alter our lives when we go back home in subtle but powerful ways. This one isn't only for moms.

I'm asking for you to come.

CHAPTER #181

Let Go to Move A Head

Last Friday I went to go hear Pixie Campbell speak about her book "Prayers of Honoring Grief".

I didn't go for the topic. I just went for Pixie, a Native American healer, teacher and writer I met at Serendipity retreat. She taught and read from passages and I teared up because UGH that my new normal is to let beauty hit me full on. Dang it.

Then she signed books and remembered me.

"This is a new look for you," referring to my hair.

I gave my two-sentence elevator pitch of loss (Without Tears Because I'm Over It). Then two sentences about cutting it all off when all I wanted was hair. This was practice for dating- short, true answers so we can move on to better subjects. Except not with Pixie.

"But it was in the middle of your divorce right?" she asked.

"Toward the end. It felt it as a public display of loss— I hated it." I admitted.

"But this is what we do— we shave our heads in mourning. The hair holds the memories. When it's cut off we can move ahead," she explained. (get it? Ahead? A head? ;-))

I had no words.

She brought me into a "we" of women who divorced, gave up hair and memories and let go only to move forward.

It was a piece I needed— to remind myself one. more. time. that I am so loved and guided and even when it (or I) look really bad, it's for a good so great I can't understand it right at that moment.

She signed my book, "Vikki- many blessings on your sacred journey! <3 Pixie"

Even though I wasn't ready to let memories go, I realize now my current length means no hair is the same before the cut.

And all of it now holds my own memories.

"Help me release my belief that I'm foolish. Replace my shame with devotion to loving from a stronger version of my heart. When I stumble again, which I will, help me find my sure—footedness and release old stories that harm my maturation and fulfillment."—Pixie Campbell

Campbell, Pixie. Prayers of Honoring Grief. Redmond: Lighthorse Publishing, 2018. P. 15.

CHAPTER #182

The Truth About Chocolate

The first 24 hours anywhere new, my fears are loud: *I'm wasting money, time, I'm not safe, and what was I thinking?*

It always surprises me. Maybe it's part of survival and healing – I don't ever remember this "travel fear" before divorce. Maybe I need proof of safety. But, leaning in, I'm learning to stretch myself and find anchors. Take extra days and put myself where I'll freak out a bit. Tell myself, "Get out of the room and just do the next thing— get dinner, or breakfast." Just fear a little less.

Wander.

Follow my What Ifs around the block... or until a chocolate shop which I passed twice before going in.

This happened in San Francisco. I'd just finished a conference nearby and decided to stay an extra three days to finally see The Golden Gate Bridge, Redwoods, trolley cars and a few friends I've missed.

My first day in, I wandered to a chocolate shop.

The owner struck up a conversation and I knew more about harvesting and selling chocolate than workers at a factory. I found a bar of Belgian chocolate and told him Id be back.

Next morning, I wasn't leaving the room (again). I remembered the chocolate shop— my safe anchor.

I'm bribing myself, "Look, it's right down the street, you won't even get lost. Besides, there's a coffee shop or three on the way."

He welcomed me back and I learned to have patience with dark chocolate, and breathe in flavor. I left with pistachio chili dark, and a 62% dark that was an imposter for milk chocolate from Italy.

Next day, I was stuck in the Airbnb room again. Again, a bribe -walk to the shop and maybe splurge on breakfast.

Somehow, between the morning fog, and steep walk downhill staring at houses built in the 1800's, I forgot to be afraid. I skipped the shop— I didn't need the anchor, the reason to get out.

Muir's redwoods were calling.

Art called that evening with Kerry Lee, an amazing artist who posted an Airbnb experience where we finished the night walking through the Door of Possibility — a collage of glass micro beads, glitter, and painted purple with the smell of hope.

Final morning I went to say goodbye to the chocolate shop and the man who it owns. I finally learned his name is Jack.

He smiled, "You'll be fine. There's lots of chocolatiers in North Carolina. And you know I ship."

I kept walking and spied a scarf impulse buy to replace one I left in the Uber. It was a scarf that I found in Italy, cotton, made in China. But I had to go back to find a shop in Florence to get it. I'd worn it every week for years because it reminded me I was already brave.

But it's gone.

I chose one that's on sale but rings up for $50.

The cashier sees my face and explains.

"You've chosen well. It's a silk scarf, that's why it's so soft. It's made in Barcelona." I sign the credit card receipt with a smile.

But left to visit with my friend Sweta at de Young art museum. Then the science museum, then dinner on 9th somewhere between the Botanical Gardens and my life in NC.

I realized I don't travel as much as I adventure— leaving room to breathe and be surprised, and ask for suggestions but let life find me between the Uber drivers and chocolate shops.

It's 5:45 am— I'm without coffee watching security guards dig through my carry on.

They pulled out my chocolates, swiping them for drugs, or something.

He smiled and promised me he put them all back in. All swipes show I'm clean, carrying nothing back with me.

Except memories, serendipity, and some hugs.

And the finest chocolate San Francisco could offer, tucked with a side of courage.

CHAPTER #183

-25-

Not In Any Order

1) Jordan is here.

2) My mom is here.

3) Great time with my dad and step mom last night over mini canoli.

4) The person who held the door for me at the post office.

5) Realizing control is different than choice.

6) Choice is always mine.

7) The wind that feels like it's blowing in all good and new.

8) Candles lit for no reason.

9) The "friendship soup" a neighbor gifted me.

10) Friends - near, far, online.

11) The moment a horse took a selfie with me just because I asked.

12) Gifts sent

13) Gifts still unwrapped

14) Doris' promise to come visit me for leftovers on Christmas day

15) Going to restorative yoga tonight - no clue what I'm in for.

16) Slow mornings with coffee and gentle sunrises

17) Accepting the things that are hard, difficult, and nonsensical without telling people to go to hell.

18) Good health.

19) Cleaning the house and the floors at one time.

20) That I bought candy canes anyway.

21) Late night talks that solve the world's problems.

22) Having extra energy because I let go.

23) That others are totally into Christmas decorating.

24) Strangers that tell me their stories - that they may be going to jail, going on vacation, going to see family, going.

25) That God always finds me.

CHAPTER #184

Paper Airplanes

I wanted a tattoo for five years, but needed to wait to get to the other side of loss before I felt I could think clearly enough for what would be meaningful.

Then my friend Kait, got a paper airplane and I didn't want to copy. I waited and asked if she was ok if I got one (not exact same) because this is a point of connection. She was great with it. But I still waited.

This past November, on Black Friday (heh), I was in a tattoo artist's chair, squeezing a worker's thick hand and apologizing for being a baby about it. They both said they understood —no apologies. They asked to tell them about the symbol, but I couldn't because I was choking back tears — not from pain but because it was the culmination of so much.

He squeezed harder.

I really needed that tattoo.

When Jordan was seven years old, we dealt with him having OCD and Tourette's and he made 61 airplanes that he hid in the closet. I felt like the worst mom ever for not knowing. I was inept. He got help. When he was in eighth grade, we were riding to the grocery store after school on country roads and he said, "It's over." I looked in the rearview mirror and said, "What's over?" He was looking out of the window and he said, "My OCD is gone. My brain is 'quiet'."

Years later, I would tell the airplane story to 1000 people. It was my chance to own all that was, get feedback, and no longer judge myself. Not one person judged me. They hugged me.

There's this Bible quote about kids being the arrows we send into the world from our quiver, and I never had a quiver... I only had one.

And I didn't even have an arrow. Or a target.

I had a paper airplane.

And instead of shooting something with aim to hit a target, I wanted something that catches the air, does loop—de—loops and sails.

I feel like that's who he is.

He was 100% on board with my choice.

It's on my right foot.

Some traditions say the right side is the one that leads, and gives versus the left which is receptive.

Other traditions say the right is the "masculine" side of the body, representing action, power, responsibility.

So, this one is also for me.

To symbolize finding and choosing the currents of life— in work, play, and adventure (not necessarily travel because adventures happen locally too).

To be okay with loop de loops.

To know I have razor edge creases that make strong sailing.

And that really, it's paper.

It can always be unfolded, reshaped and launched again.

So, on Black Friday, I sat in a tattoo artist's chair and reframed the pieces of my life that mean the most, and with a hand to hold.

CHAPTER #185

So Proud of You, Mom

Many of you have kids who graduated or are moving up from elementary to middle, or middle to high school.

Many of you are trying to figure out how to wrap your head around college in the Fall, or these being the last 4 years of school, or eyeing the empty nest next year.

So, I wanted to reach out and tell you *Yes, Congratulations for your kids! They did it!*

But really, I see you.

I see that you are trying very hard to let go or accept that they are no longer babies and that time is so fast.

I see that you're trying to stay in their lives while letting them flutter.

And I really see that there is no line of cards or gifts for parents when their child accomplishes so much and you were in the supporting role the.whole.time.

And where's the necklace, or ring or card that hands us over to this next season?

Where's the ceremony that says we're moving forward too?

I get it.

And so this is for you... as you're trying to sort your own life as they sort theirs. As you're trying to figure out hands off/ hands on and time just barrels on. As you don't know if you should offer a hug or just a shoulder.

I so get this.

And here's what I know.

You matter. You always have. You still do.

Actually, nothing was possible without you.

So, if you're saying goodbye to that elementary hallway for the last time, or the middle school football field, or the high school rhythms, there's no way through except to grieve the loss.

And let it transition itself in it's own time.

It's o.k.a.y to feel a lack of gravity, and trying to sort the "no mores" and the "not yets" of the next school year.

And it's o.k.a.y to be okay.

This takes time and you will as soon as your heart and brain can find the north star again, you will make sense of this.

But until then, soak up this summer with them.

Count the moments and the fireflies.

Ask questions, and journal moments and laugh so hard you can't breathe.

You always have and always will matter.

You gave them life and now you give them wings for their next stage.

Much, much love.

CHAPTER #186

Following Breadcrumbs -Part 1

When I was 16, I spent a summer with a Japanese family in Yokosuka. I'd won a scholarship sponsored by both governments and Youth for Understanding. Only two students from every state in the US got to go. Somehow, they chose me.

When I arrived at their house, it was like I came home. We had the best summer ever.

Their last name was mother's, Okasan's, maiden name as her lineage was shogun.

At one point, Otosan (father) showed me a family sword and explained it was at least 500 years old.

Then he showed me a warrior arrow — wooden, with feathers at the end — and asked me if I liked it.

I carefully said it was beautiful.

But he asked me again if I liked it.

In Japanese culture, if you say you like something, it is to be given to you. I knew this was their heirloom and legacy. I didn't want to offend but somehow could not accept this gift.

But he looked sad, "Vikki—san. You don't like?"

"No, I love it, but its' yours."

Then it was mine. Handed over.

It was a long amazing summer with my sisters Akiko and Nahomi —— school, art lessons, and ultimately, I jogged alone from our home to the Colonel Matthew C. Perry monument at Yokosuka beach by myself.

Long story short, when the summer ended, the arrow didn't fit in my suitcase. At the last minute, I asked that they keep "my" arrow with them so when I come back to visit, I can see it again, along with my rice bowl and chopsticks. ;-)

I returned four years later for a visit. We were family.

But then we lost touch in the undertow of life.

Last year, when I was piecing days together, looking for what I knew to be true, in the midst of healing grief, I wrote a letter to their old address, searched to find them and Google mapped the path from the house to the Perry monument.

I couldn't find them.

Probably, the girls got married and changed their names. Maybe Okasan and Otosan died. If they were alive, and near the house, they would have written back. They would have found me. I wrote on my wall that I used to piece life together, "Japan- 1986."

CHAPTER #187

Following Breadcrumbs -Part 2

I was finding ways to ground myself in life again. So, while I was in Portland, my friend Shannon took me on a day trip to Cannon Beach. The truth about Shannon is, we were there ten years ago with families that look very different now. Our husbands were friends. Our North Carolina family visited the year we homeschooled Jordan because of OCD and Tourette's. Our kids – her four at the time, and my one- played at Cannon Beach.

In time, they fractured.

In more time, so did we.

Except Shannon and I stayed in each other's periphery. It was a perfect place to come full circle with our friendship intact.

We ended up in a treasure hunter's shop where they would tell you the story of anything you were interested in.

We circled the shop.

I landed on a one-inch teeny tiny piece of silver with Kanji (Chinese stylized writing).

"Oh. This is one of our most interesting pieces. A long time ago, Japanese samurai swords held secret compartments in the bottom where they kept pieces of silver. When Colonel Matthew Perry landed in Nagasaki, he opened Japan to the West for trade, and often these swords were used to barter."

"But he didn't open the west until he got to Yokosuka. There's a monument at the beach," I entered. "Where is this silver piece from?"

"We got this from Yokosuka. Maybe samurai or shogun were fishing, or they traded their swords and boats sank and we found them." She finished and I knew it was mine.

If this was all I had to symbolize my Japanese family then it was enough. Pieces of life come together in bits. I figured if I had enough bits, they would have to make up something of a life.

About 3 months later, I woke up on a Saturday morning and a Japanese name messaged me on Facebook. "Hi Vikki! This is Akiko from Japan. I'm using my daughter's IPhone...."

I was stunned.

As I started typing a response, they called.

My Japanese was horrible. Her English was amazing.

The parents were still alive.

They'd been looking for me.

She got married and he kept the matriarchal name.

She became an English teacher and married a teacher who is now a principal.

She had 2 girls.

I told her I was an English teacher who married a teacher and we are no longer married. I had one boy.

They were coming to visit Los Angeles.

I said Jordan just moved from LA.

We were already intertwining each other's lives again.

At some point, we will visit and condense decades into days.

I have been willing to follow breadcrumbs to a new life. It's been weird. It's not my normal "charge" style. But it's taught me to look twice around me, be in the moment, receive the gifts all the pieces because it's really a mosaic.

Always has been.

Now when I look back at the trail, they aren't breadcrumbs at all. They are gold nuggets and silver pieces on a really wide path saying, "This is the way, keep going" with Otosan's kind smile telling me as he always did, "Vikki—san. Just try."

CHAPTER #188

Meatballs and Henna

Last week on social media I saw a local refugee organization created a festival to celebrate World Refugee Day.

But it was the same organization that I called last year twice to volunteer and didn't get a call back. I ignored it.

So I went to a coffee shop and as I poured cream and looked down, there was a flyer for the exact same festival. They were making it a potluck, with food from around the world.

I'm getting good at this and don't need another nudge. Next stop was for frozen meatballs and Sweet Baby Ray's BBQ sauce and some Hawaiian rolls because apparently, they need some hometown love.

You would think I'd have a little more trust and confidence at this stage, but I never do. I've decided contingency plans are always my bravest choice.

I invited Jordan who declined. He asked what I expected when I went. Wistfully I replied, "I want to meet people from far flung places — Eritrea, Yemen, Bali, Myanmar— I don't know. But if I can't get in and talk to people, I'll just bring them food and leave. No big deal. But I think I need to be there."

There were about 200 people— 2/3 were refugees.

Some were citizens.

And there was henna.

After I spent awhile talking to the organizers, (and warning about pork in the meatballs I brought because I TOTALLY forgot about religious restrictions), I sat for henna.

I would wear henna on both hands all summer long if I could. I've thought about tattoing permanent henna designs on my hands I love it so much.

Her work was amazing. She was from Yemen. Majored in English.

She became a citizen just last week.

She said that everyone told her she was crazy, that it couldn't happen, but she said if God decided she fails, then at least she tried. But she was going to try.

An 11-year-old boy from Mexico stood by to watch her.

I looked around. He was blended in with other kids in a parking lot filled with people from Cambodia, Vietnam, Congo, Eritrea, Ethiopia, Yemen, Syria. They came to our airport with their lives and little else, fleeing religious, or political persecution.

Phones were a rare commodity. Kids were running around, laughing, playing ball. Adults were, eating, talking and videoing when the Arabic community did a line dance, or the Congolese choir sang.

I called my friend, Sabrina, who came. We sat and ate authentic Vietnamese noodles, and Eritrean bread, and other dishes we knew were made with love. She wanted to leave a donation- but I brought food to cover us. She seemed uneasy because she just got off of work – in the food industry- where nothing is free. Nothing. I told her that this was to truly celebrate people who came here with nothing, not to raise money. Relationships here are not based on what you buy or give. It's based, for tonight, on presence, and celebrating, and joining in.

I am a very tiny person in a very hurting world. All I wanted to do is what has been done for me over the course of my life when I traveled — welcome, share food, stumble over language, and love hard. If I didn't fit in and left, that would have been ok because I wanted to bring food.

I think love counts.

But loving harder for me means getting over just a bit the fear in my head, and showing up. From there, it's just jumping in and looking at people's joy and pain while eating Cambodian salad and talking to the teen girls from the Congo with Middle Eastern pop playing in the background.

CHAPTER #189

The Goal

Every vacation I take a bit of time and scan for blind spots, or things I've not listened to. It sounds weird, and I can't explain it other than I get super quiet and ask what's been coming up that I haven't been listening to.

The answer this time was about three broken hearts.

Over the past few months, its' come up in conversation with people who are free to tell me anything, that they feel I still have a broken heart.

The first time, I was like, "OMG. I need to heal. What do you do to heal a broken heart as quickly as possible?" But there were no quick answers, so I forgot about it.

Then it came up twice more.

On the final time I said to the friend, "But so what if I do still have a broken heart?"

Truth is, I've *not* been focusing on my heart.

Or healing.

I've really been dreaming, taking steps on building a life, rooting out fear in all forms, honoring losses, listening to my body, and rebuilding.

I've not sat around saying "Now let's focus on healing a broken heart."

In a super safe space on vacation, I needed to revisit that. Maybe I'm supposed to address this? My whole life other people's opinions have been more truthful than my own. In my new life, they are not. But three times, so I dove in.

Here's where I'm landing...

I live in a world where the goal of what's broken is to fix it, good as new, moving toward ultimate wholeness and even happiness. Here's the self-help equation (valued at $99):

As soon as I (buy, heal, fix) so that (good things happen, success, happiness) because until then I'm (not as valued, less than, broken, unhappy).

But A+ B isn't C.

Crazier yet, I didn't break my heart. If I did, I would know how to fix it. So neither can I heal it on command. ;-)

I started scanning my life for clues. Last year around this exact time, I got a second degree burn on my arm that probably I need to consider about now…

The doctor told me how to take care of it——not heal it.

Use antibacterial wash 3-4 times a day.

Air it out.

Wrap it and protect it.

Truth is, I didn't heal my arm. I created the environment for it to heal. I didn't devalue my arm, or think it was of no use to me. It didn't disqualify me from doing anything.

Most days it didn't look like it was healing, and it took longer than I really wanted. But I could trust my body implicitly to work in secret dark places where I can't see, control, or force anything to happen.

All I could do is create the environment for healing to happen.

Eventually, I saw the results of all that hidden work — new layers of skin deliberately sealing itself.

Yep — there was a scar for a long time.

Even better was a story that went with it.

Good as new? Not really. We like things unblemished, and yet the scars make things more interesting.

At this point, there is almost no scar, but it's taken a year. I decided at the beach that no doubt there's still missing pieces and cracks, but not nearly as many as last year, or three years ago.

But that's not really what I value.

I value creating the environment for healing — the working on dreams, adventuring even just to get a cup of coffee, living through fear and practicing intuition as a way of life.

I think if others have opinions on a heart being broken or not, that's great. I just don't share them.

Because I know very clearly to not disturb or judge or look at things while they are layers deep, doing magic and miracles just because I keep doing the things that help support the healing... in this case, to keep showing up.

Because the goal isn't really to hurry up and heal.

The goal is to have a life. ;-)

CHAPTER #190

Let It

I got a tattoo on my arm on Black (ink) Friday last year. The paper airplane is easier to understand. This one I have explained really poorly to people...so I'm going to lean on the Karate Kid for this one.

Its' one of my favorite movies ever. But there's a scene that feels like life and I'm finally bowing. Finally.

Mr. Miyagi (returning from fishing and explaining why Daniel wasn't invited): "You karate training."

Daniel: "I'm being your goddamn slave is what I'm being. Now we made a deal here.

Mr. Miyagi: So?

D: So You're supposed to teach me and I'm supposed to learn, remember? For four days I've been busting my ass over every little goddamn thing.

M: You learned plenty.

D: I learned plenty. I've learned how to sand your decks maybe.. I've learned how to wash your car, paint your house, paint your fence, yeah, I've learned plenty.

M: Ah. No difference. Not everything is as it seems.

D: Ah bullshit. I'm going home, man.

M: Daniel—san, Daniel—san come here. Show me sand the floor.

D: I can't move my arm, alright?

(Mr. Miyagi does energy work on his shoulder)

M: Now show me sand the floor… big sucker – sand the floor..... now show me wax on wax off... show me paint the fence... look eye—always look eye... (they face off)… Come back tomorrow.

Grief, loss, facing fear and learning showing up have asked me to paint fences and sand floors, wax on and wax off. And, honestly, my soul is kinda sore and worn out.

I've been pissed and tired.

It's been a lot of bullshit and I'm ready to go back to doing life the way I always did — control, stress, force without power— because this way isn't "working". Where the F is my life? Where's the end already?

All I could do was *let it…* go, come, be, stay, leave, show up, in, out. So the tattoo I have – because I have to stay very open – is "*let it."* I've not really understood at all what training it's been. What I have been trusting is to keep showing up, do the next thing and above all remember that things aren't always as they seem. I have been trusting that implicitly.

Here's the link to the scene where Daniel-san puts everything in practice, swinging hard. https://bit.ly/2GeUkR9

So I'm swinging hard now...fielding the fast throws. I'm here and finally getting it, sorta. With a *let it* tattoo, and a deep bow, knowing for sure more is coming, but that the training is stored in my muscles. Trusting and believing that now, as the bigger challenges come with a life well lived, that they'll be met eye to eye and with hidden sharp stealth, samurai fierce grace, and a quiet trust that not everything is always as it seems.

It's often mind-blowingly better. And always, to come back tomorrow.

CHAPTER #191

Starting to Date

Last week in my online dating debut, in the midst of a flurry of "new girl on the dating site" contacts received, I got disoriented.

After sifting through messages with photos that were not attractive to me, I kindly replied I was not interested. I was left with a handful of, "Hey sexy's" and a few, "Nice smiles."

After several days of this I was tired, overwhelmed, and disappointed.

Really, all I want to do is meet someone because I helped some guy at the grocery store find a greeting card for his sister's new baby because he's out of town on work..and spark.

So I backed up to how I was treating people. Because judgment, and criticism takes it's toll on me... and where was gratitude? And what's with all the married men? What am I attracting here?

So I shifted hard left... back to who and how I want to be— everything I've been learning — finding the sacred, trusting myself, being grateful and respectful. Taking full on responsibility for the energy I'm bringing to a space, even my profile.

How can I show up in this situation without criticism, but honoring myself?

Passing on men became a silent gratitude, "No, but thank you."

If they messaged me with respect, I would respond even if they were in Ireland or Italy... and ask a question of their profile. Usually they didn't respond back. Apparently, a little honest engagement shuts down the sex drive or the catfisher.

I ignored all messages starting, "Hey sexy."

I wanted the married men to go away, and realized my profile pic had sunglasses... and I didn't talk about work. Truth is, I was hiding, because I was nervous to be on there... and I'm thinking that was sending out "hiding" signals, maybe. So I changed my profile pic, and talked about work I love. Only one "like" since then from a "non-monogamous" man.

The day after all these changes, everything slowed down. And some answers popped up— look for the men vs. the boys, only go for profiles with faces, trust your instinct.

If I want men, how do I show up as a woman versus a girl? How can I keep integrity with myself as a human while still searching for a date? (I've notched down from Love for now) .

I never wanted to slam the entire male population for what a few boys are doing online (regardless of their age). I want to stay in a place of respect — it's hard for men too. It's hard to message someone, even if you bumble it. But if I can respect them, myself and the process maybe this will feel different. Because the mystery man from Turkey who wanted me to marry him and be his queen deserved a respectful decline. And even "magical sex elf" wrote a response to a question for what he most wants: connection.

I needed connection too. But not like this.

So, I went to see how Doris was next door.

And snagged dinner with Jordan

And wrote posts for my blog.

Later that evening, I came back to a message about one of my photos, "What covered bridge are you in?" and from there... I have a date for Saturday. The first in four years since I had a blind date and decided to go *momagamous*— choosing parenting over dating.

I have no clue what I'm doing.

But if I can figure out what I'm not doing, then clearing that away gives me a forward path... and for now it's more than enough.

What I'm not doing is anything that veers from this beautiful, crazy, wild path I'm on that is apparently my new normal of life. A little sacred, a whole lot of "let it", and a smidge of wth?

CHAPTER #192

Shifting Back Into Neutral

A few weeks ago I needed an oil change. I also asked for them to check everything over because I was driving a lot.

An hour later, I'm under my car being shown tires that are nearly bald in the front. Back tires are curved square.

Apparently, I needed shocks about 30,000 miles ago.

And an alignment.

So, the oil change turned into four new tires, shocks, oil change, cabin filter, and alignment.

Hours later, as I was paying I joked, "You know, this was just supposed to be an oil change."

I saw his face shift down.

He started to defend the cost. Everything shifted.

So I decided to shift it back.... wondering if it were even possible.

"So, can I just tell you something? You guys saved my butt. I was riding on square tires. You've helped me sign up for a card that will give me back $125. You're giving me free tire rotation and alignments. You offered to move the square tires up front to save me money. Winter is coming and new tires would double as snow tires too. That car has 125,000 miles and I've never replaced the shocks. As far as I can tell, I've got nothing to complain about and everything to be grateful for. You're not charging me, I'm buying them. I'm choosing all this. So, thank you, Derrick. And will you thank the two guys who worked on the car as well? "

The other mechanic at the register stopped what he was doing. Nobody said anything.

Everything shifted.

I don't know.

Maybe it's so little it doesn't matter.

But maybe just noticing can matter.

I'm trying to be more aware...of people around me, of situations, of energy, of interactions, of shifting, of engaging well. I hope one day I can be involved in really helping someone because I was aware of something happening...but for now, just one interaction at a time can count for something.

CHAPTER #193

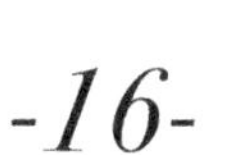

-16-

The Gratitude List Just for Today

1. A little clarity on next steps after a long season of gray
2. The rain that held off then let loose- both.
3. The fireflies every single night
4. Sinking into bed after a day of giving 100%
5. Jordan being home for now
6. Finding perfect gifts
7. Finding bits of myself that were familiar that I thought were gone
8. Not shrinking back from potential conflict, only to work through it with truth and love
9. When questions finally get answers even though you forgot about ever wondering
10. Wanting what you want.
11. Saying "Not Now."
12. Saying "I can't".
13. Trying to figure out FearLessFridays as a book while feeling completely flattened remembering all the love those posts got.
14. Friends. Wherever they are.
15. New music for the gym.
16. When people message you and say "This is so hard" because they know you get it.

CHAPTER #194

That Thing About Apology

I didn't apologize growing up. No one in our house apologized. I've asked my mom about this to see if I missed something and she said, "What would we apologize for?"

Heh.

Forgiveness, however, was expected — given without anyone ever asking.

So, I grew up (to my recollection) where anyone could do anything and you never had to apologize and were always forgiven.

On the other hand....you were expected to never need an apology and just forgive.

Marriage changed that.

Having a son changed that.

Although I am trained from birth as a ninja forgiver, apologizing has taken next level intervention.

Enter my friend Dr. Jennifer McCain Thomas. She co—authored a book on apology with Dr. Gary Chapman called, *When Sorry Isn't Enough*.

Jen and I are real life friends. I've talked with her at length over cans of whipped cream (which I totally replace next visit), about how HARD IT IS to apologize....how powerful it is to teach our kids to do this without shame... how most public apologies are lacking...and on and on. Like, hours.

Recognizing my extreme deficit, I've busted hard applying her work for about seven years. I now find apology one of the most powerful, respected, rarest things on the planet. Any form of apology anyone ever offers me is an act of uncommon courage. Every relationship I've had that failed— I intentionally gave a no holds barred apology — whether it could be saved or not— I wanted to go clear, nothing left unspoken. Apologies with agenda are manipulation... don't ask me how I learned that one.

Some of the failed relationships were with dear friends. Sometimes we were both trying to save our own lives amidst divorce and ended up hurting each other through a convoluted misunderstanding. Sometimes I let them down or they let me down and the hurt was too deep to patch. Sometimes, amidst my own transitions, I didn't have the energy to fight to save any of them. Other times I think, "If I just tried harder."

Last week was another round of personal forgiveness that I do to stay clear, not bitter, and grateful... I literally sit and ask if I'm holding hurt or grudge against anyone. There's always someone. Then, I "talk" with them...releasing, thanking, finding love as best I can— which always feels feeble, but just enough. Then I "apologize" to them. Imagining the hurt I've caused, from their perspective, helps me to own my role in our demise, even when they aren't around.

Our culture HYPES forgiveness. But it misses an initial apology. Jen and I have intensely discussed this over driving to pick up kids or dining room tables, about her work juxtaposing culture. How we're expected, as I was growing up, to forgive without someone owning what they did.

And yet, forgiveness is effortless when someone initiates, owns their part, and says 'I apologize'.

She's talked with Dr. Chapman, author of *The 5 Love Languages*, about authentic apology being the 6th, Universal, Love Language. Globally and across cultures there is no other interaction like it in function and scope.

I've landed on forgiveness as a necessary, personal decision to try to heal what was done to me. It's the only tool I have when another won't or can't engage with me.

It's incredibly powerful.

But authentic apology, not one given so someone can clear their own guilt because caught, but because a wrong was done and there's remorse, changes the inhale and exhale of two people.

——Jen's work can be found here: https://www.drjenniferthomas.com/

CHAPTER #195

Grinding the Grindstone

Last week was some news of another imminent loss that sent me hiking on a new trail at Pilot Mountain. I planned for about a two hour hike, stopped at the ranger's office, got clear on the trail at 1.8 miles according to them, and knew to stay right at the forks and it would end up at the parking lot. I had water and took off with deep respect for this sacred land, needing to leave some burdens there.

Once I got there, the sign said 2.2 miles. I went anyway.

The views at 2400 feet were breathtaking. My steps were slower than I expected, because the hike started with descending stone steps at two feet each. Didn't care. Needed to breathe.

Somewhere around the rock climbing walls, I started asking people on the trail how much further. Some didn't know because they dropped in from the top, so their point of view wasn't mine.

Some could only tell me when the road smoothed out that I would be about halfway. One told me what would be the truth: when the road smoothed out, I still had 1.2 miles to go.

Time in a wooded forest is inert. The only way you can really tell is by the sun or your phone if there's a signal. I lost signal. Ultimately, the road smoothed out as the sun lowered. My body was spent, and fighting a migraine for awhile. I'd been juice fasting to detox for two days and didn't expect the severity of this hike. Here, my phone signal returned— two and half hours in.

I sat and drank water but as I cooled down, my energy sank more. It's funny how in a critical situation you can't evaluate clearly. Do I keep going or go back? I knew what was behind me and I couldn't go up what I just scaled down. The path was smooth ahead but at 1.2 miles, I didn't have it in me— fear set in.

So I started the self-talk I'm familiar with: *Let me guess, this is a lesson.. I got myself into this and I can't get out. I shouldn't have done this. This is what I do, I jump and then look*. But none of that was true --I did talk to rangers, I asked questions, I had water.

I stopped myself. I'd been learning how to shift, to just fear a tiny bit less, so I tried it: *It's Pilot freaking Mountain, I'm not dying here. Just be in it. Just feel and breathe. Trust.*

I breathed into it enough to not regret this. No matter what. I needed every step, and watching every inspiring woman climbing on that rock face. The oncoming loss was triggering emotional survival again and the trail helped shake me out of control. I will never again regret doing what I really wanted just because I got into it and hit the point of, "Oh sh*&." Without regret, or doubt, everything got very, very still for me. I saw the trees. The way the path changed. Just sitting.

Another Voice said, "What do you need?"

And I said out loud, "I need food. I'm so hungry. I really messed up not taking food."

Within five minutes a couple came by, and we small chatted — they weren't prepared for this either. I said, "Hey, when you get to the split, stay right." They walked away but the woman turned around and said, "Hey, do you want a Cliff bar?"

I didn't even get up, I was in disbelief.

"I have an extra Cliff bar and Gu, ever heard of that?"

I got up.

Gu is a fast absorbing energy gel with amino acids, and caffeine. I took both. They walked away and I cried.

Mostly because I was heard.

And to not blame myself for following my heart even if I need help halfway.

And because I realized help is what I came here for and sometimes

I forget to ask because I'm trying to power through. I can ask earlier.

In total, I hiked 4.5 hours. No pain in my back or knees.

I drove home the long way, which meant on the back roads where I used to live. Familiar world.

A guy was walking with a gas can, sweaty, no car in sight and I picked him up. It's what we do on those roads.

He couldn't believe I stopped. As he got gas, I looked down at the Gu wrapper. We're all in it together. His truck was 1.5 miles away, his girlfriend waiting for him.

This life is not what I know. Following my heart, my path, the mountains, will always put me in unfamiliar territory. But going back isn't really an option, is it?

I may even have to ask for help.

So be it.

Because when I do, and come out on the other side, I can give a ride to others. That's the life I really want.

CHAPTER #196

At Home

The dating thing...

Although it's true that online dating has been aggressive and treacherous (at best), it's also been beautiful to watch the response of friends messaging to not settle.

And yet the online world has given me much needed practice for what I'm clear on— what will I give a free pass to?

What will I tolerate now?

What will I stand for?

What matters in the way I'm respected and treated even after a few messages?

My "No" pile is really large.

I'm not willing to carry the entire conversation. Nor compliment in every sentence. Nor disappear into their life, cooking their food, making their coffee, asking how their day was, and completing them.... unless it's very, very reciprocated in terms we both agree on. I've learned that if I have to "help them understand" what I mean, it's easier to block and delete rather than accepting a dynamic of me explaining myself because they are offended, confused, or manipulative.

No, I don't believe I'm "attracting" the questionable men... I believe, if anything, it's my opportunity to flex my "oh heck no" signal for what is not acceptable in my space.

I know that ease and grace exist, even though strength and fight and push are the relationship muscle memory on default. Ease of connection, I will always believe, is essential.

The waiting to date after a season of transition has only made me stronger, clearer, stealthier, smarter, and more willing to not settle... so what's a little more waiting?

I am home in my life.

I'm not waiting to start living once he arrives. Actually, this week I learned (again) that by choosing my life each day, I'm inherently eliminating the men who want me to complete them, sit home with them, retire with them.

Because I'm clear on my path.

And they will have to either be on that path already or be ok that I'm on it.

And we all know, when I do meet The Guy, it's going to be the best FearLessFriday ever, no matter how it ultimately happens.

CHAPTER #197

To the Mommas Saying Goodbye

Mom, maybe this finds you driving home from a campus.

Or dropping them off at an airport because all they wanted was a gap year across the country – or the world.

It might be your first, last or only child. Either way, you're crossing a threshold that we don't often talk about: launching into adulthood.

It's a passage from one world to another.

Logically, we're happy. We WANTED this day. We are DONE. No more conflict, biting our tongue, wondering if we've done enough, or buying extra snacks in case friends come over after school.

Done.

I did this two years ago when Jordan wanted a gap year in Los Angeles. He returned a year later.

But now he's returning to the west coast, giving me a three-week notice.

Having been through this before, I want to tell you a few things so you don't feel crazy or like there's something wrong with you. Hardly.

After the initial tears and get-on-with-the-day, there's this morning of waking up and it's one less voice in the house. You might cry at breakfast because you know exactly how to make their eggs and they aren't here.

Maybe you need to pull the car over because you realized you passed their school.

Or as you make dinner, it's ok if you need to use the dishtowel because tissues can't hold the tears when you realize it's. Every. Single. Dinner. that you won't be making for them again.

You may find yourself vacuuming just to stay busy and remembering all the times you thought an empty house is what you wanted- and now you want them back.

And you can't have them back.

So, you think about when you'll see them next— holidays or breaks. Or go visit.

But I need to warn you. You'll need a minute to recognize them. Because they'll have outgrown the image in your heart of them at age five or nine or 14 or even 18.

So, we can't have them back as we knew them.

Neither can we have back the season of mothering we just walked through.

This deserves the honor of tears.

Because you, momma, did an unspeakably amazing job and they are flying. Solo. Without you. As you've been planning on for nearly two decades. Now, they carry you with them— your wit and intelligence and height. And you carry them in every cell of your heart.

The thing is, there most likely will be this unexpected day where you feel like you are on an elevator going down. And you won't know what to do. Or what you're supposed to do. But I have a few ideas and I'm hoping you'll join me as we walk this one together. Ok?

We're going to feel into the new normal.

They were our world and our world is somewhere else. And it can feel disembodying.

So, we will let it. And we'll cry – or not.

We'll take a week to decide if going in their room is possible or not. Or a month to figure out if we really want dinner at 6pm when there's no soccer practice at 7pm.

Together, we will resist texting them more than once in a day.

And we pinky swear to never ever ask them if they're eating well, who their friends are or what grade they got on an exam. We will let them carve the life with all the trust and elbow room they need.

Maybe we'll find some cards and send notes to their friends that are no longer coming over laughing and playing video games or making videos or snapchatting other friends.

And we'll resist zoning out on screens – we told them to be in the real world, and now we need this reminder.

So, we'll journal.

Or find the photos we took for so many years.

We'll go through the scrapbooks or boxes – this is why we saved that favorite shirt when they were seven. Or the baby teeth. Or their kindergarten handprints. This is the "one day" we saved it for.

We're honoring all that we walked.

And when we can't breathe we'll go outside, and let the sun and air and sky breathe for us.

Together, we're going to trust the emotional wave only lasts 2—12 minutes… apparently, the longer the wave, the bigger the dish towel to cry into. I found that sitting with it, and not distracting myself even though it all seems bigger than me— that it's not bigger than me. Or you.

That we are equal to it.

And with a little prayer, maybe even bigger than the waves we thought would overtake us.

The secret is, leaning in and grieving instead of distraction and numbing, means we will find our new life.

One day, the tears will be only sometimes — usually at bedtime because they aren't there to say goodnight.

And maybe we'll decide that we want big lunches and tiny dinners.

And we'll have extra money to buy that pricey bar of chocolate the one with the chili in it perfectly grounded.

And maybe we'll cry because no one is there to share it or a spouse doesn't understand. But just for a bit.

And maybe the Monet exhibit is still on at the art museum and we can read every.single.description.

A month will pass by and our iPhone photos are starting to build a life that is very different from the previous one. But look: smiling selfies and maybe even some with a spouse or boyfriend or kids that are home. It all counts.

At some point we may look through clothes and wonder how long we've had the sweats that don't have a drawstring anymore— and now there's time and money to go find a new pair without getting stuck at the mall for hours.

Maybe you realize can get one drink at Starbucks and not one for everyone.

Or you start to think about a trip you wanted to take. Or the divorce you wanted. Or the fully stocked bar you always dreamed of. Or the new boyfriend you now deserve.

And I'm asking you to wait.

Just wait.

Get on the other side of loss. Finish honoring one season before charging into the next one.

Of course, you're an adult and can do what you want. But loss is a wild friend that plays hide and seek and pounces when you thought it was over. And you'll think you're fine, really. You're not crying all.the. time anymore.

You're good.

And I offer to wait just a little longer…

How long do you wait?

As long as it takes until you can talk about your child, go in their room, wash their sheets, and not cry while doing it.

...until you can remember how they used to jump on the bed and you yelled for them to stop, and not cry thinking about it.

....until you can go through the family photos— and remember how you fought depression for so long and realize no one would ever know because the only thing you see now is the love.

And you'll really know it's time when you see it's 9pm, and decide to take a bath and read a book and not cry because the house is so quiet.

Because here's the other secret— (pinky swear).

They will come back.

And your heart will breathe again, but a little differently.

And they'll need a minute to recognize you because you have a life without them.

You aren't yelling or frazzled or hurrying to pack lunches at 9pm at night.

You have time to talk to them.

And listen.

And laugh again.

And realize that you were the mom you always hoped you were.

And so much more.

Because the person sitting before you is stunning. And grown and growing.

And you recognize them completely, and parts you are longing to rediscover and learn.

And you thought you couldn't love them more and now you realize you can and do.

And that they are so much more than you ever dreamed.

Because they demanded you to be so much more than you ever thought – and after 18 years you are that amazing.

You will feel into the next ebb and flow of breaks and summers and visits and perfectly imperfect Christmases where you decide no tree because you're tired and they want one anyway and they will put it up for you.

But it all depends on you leaning in.

Letting loss and grief mix with honor and grace for the life you had, and the season you sacrificially loved beyond yourself. Because when you build a life from that place, you have the life you really do deserve— one you built with love.

And maybe now, instead of that divorce, it's counseling or a separation.

Instead of that new fully stocked bar, it's a girls night out once a week.

And maybe now truly full speed ahead for the boyfriend (***raising my hand).

Because as life settles, you'll only have space for what is a high act of love for your life.

Because now it is about you, and from a place of love, not fear and loss and grief.

And you have honored your season and know the worth and weight of your life in tears, sleepless nights, and laughter. And you move into this next phase, may it be with grace, and courage and a wild knowing that although you can't hug them every day, they are still your world.

CHAPTER #198

Waterproof Eyeliner and Toilet Brushes

Three weeks ago, Jordan visited Los Angeles.

In the middle of that week, a breathtaking painting arrived unexpectedly.

This painting started in March when my online friend Tammy Lynn asked for feather stories for a blog she was thinking about. She requested to just send her a photo of a feather and why it's meaningful to you.

So, I sent a story of this feather that appeared at the front door the week Jordan came back home. I kept it because it was a young goose feather -half adult and half down- ready for the world, but layers underneath still forming.

In the four months while she was painting, things were taking flight here.

The painting showed up. A wispy white half-down, half-feather swirling against a turquoise-ombre background. It is the color of all art in my living room even though she knew nothing of my color scheme.

Within days of the new art, the call came from Jordan, "I'm moving back out here."

The three-week countdown is now a 12 hour countdown and all I really want to do is to escape to the places I hike even though its' in the middle of the night.

Or ride a stationary bike past my standard 40-minutes at the gym.

Or be halfway to Asheville by now, windows down, Kenny Chesney's songs on repeat.

But Jordan is gone for the day and inadvertently in a miscommunication took both sets of keys.

So, I'm resisting making a batch of chocolate pudding or going back to sleep.

I'm landing on the two choices I have and really, the only two choices that matter. The ones that have guided me these past few years: Will I trust? Will I show up?

For me, I translate it as *will I trust that God was giving me clues and sending me love before I needed it?*

Can I trust that things are brewing without me knowing and they will converge and conspire on my behalf for an amazing life? Even when it looks like another loss? And will I show up?

To the toilets that need scrubbing.

To the clothes piles frozen in time.

To the papers cluttering the desk about the retreat.

To the six ways to Sunday I'm behind on writing.

And in the showing up to another loss, will I do it with tears and wholeheartedly? Will I resist thinking that washing clothes or cooking dinner or just being here when he comes home is *not enough*?

He leaves tomorrow before the sun comes up.

His feathers are further along than the painting shows. But so are my own. Maybe somehow we can both soar now, in different ways, trusting all we needed was a little more time, growth, and love. And clean laundry.

Because it's always in the practical daily bits where the dreams and plans are made for the next right choice.

That and trusting the next steps appear always.

I mean, if a painting in the works for four months is perfectly colored and timed to land —what other perfect timings are right around the corner? ;-)

Tammy Lynn's beautiful blog is www.TheLanguageOfFeathers.com

CHAPTER #199

Just Wear a T-Shirt and Jeans

I've been attempting to date.

"Attempting" because some want to only message. Or during messaging they just stop communicating. Or if you do finally meet, it's a 45 minute "interview" complete with them asking, "Is there anything else you want to know about me?" and you realized most of what you did was talk about them.

I'm not sure what happened to a round of miniature golf and a coffee, but holy moly.

So I decided no more "interviews." Clearly, I've been complicit in this process. The trick has been to figure out how. I had a few dates coming up and thought I'd at least see if I could change my part.

I was up front with both of them — no interview. Please don't dress up for me, I had my favorite T shirt and jeans picked out. That eliminated half my problem right there. I would show up as myself. The only person I was going home with was me.

I was trying to impress or earn attention and that would stop immediately. I spent a little time finding the things I'm impressed with myself about. And sorted in my head that their attention is the bonus to my friends and life — not the be all end all goal.

I would stop right here right now ever again proving my worth of attention to any man. For me that translates into not finding them the most fascinating person in the room at all times, not listening more than speaking, and not impressing them with anything, even where my favorite food on the planet is. (By the way— hot dogs all the way at my friend Michelle's canteen, South on Bostwick, in Bridgeport, Connecticut at noon on any work day).

Hmmm. But if they didn't like me at the end of just being myself, THEN WHAT????

Well, what if that wasn't the goal?

What if I went with love already for myself? Heh.

What if, more radically, I went to love them— and THEY didn't have to prove anything either?

Then what would happen?

No clue, but anything was better than the 45 min. interview, pelted with questions, and them always coming up short.

Here's what I learned.

They wore JEANS. And laughed.

My questions were different, and so were theirs. We talked about moments and hard choices and places that were failures. They told me more truthful stories and about their lives than I ever would have learned pelting them with questions or vice versa.

One date was 4.5 hours.

Another was 2.5 hours.

Hours.

Plans for more dates.

A few days later I realized neither naturally had a few essentials I really needed. Not because they were failures, or not enough, or didn't check boxes.

But because I couldn't bear to change a thing about them.

Maybe that's the gift in love, to let people be who they are and not prove themselves. Just be.

From there the only decision is, "Do I want to just be with this person?"

There are no further dates with either.

They remain the men who taught me about love — for men and for myself, equally. They showed me how jeans and T-shirts are completely perfect for first dates. And to never prove myself. And to always accept others before they do anything to earn it.

Mostly, myself.

CHAPTER #200

The Only Impossibility

"There is only one thing that makes a dream impossible to achieve: the fear of failure."

— Paulo Coelho

Coelho, Paulo. The Alchemist. San Francisco: HarperSanFrancisco, 1998. Print. p. 135.

CHAPTER #201

Karaoke On Tap

You don't know who your long haul friends are until there's a long haul.

When it was the hardest, she texted me nearly every morning, "All you need to do is get up and make the coffee."

Leslie, self-proclaimed introvert, unafraid to match pink with anything, mom of two boys and my friend for 20 years, is going through a difficult life shift.

She had a birthday this week which I knew was not going to be fun, so several weeks ago we planned to get together.

She decided on karaoke.

You may be able to tell, but I don't know how to navigate the bar scene very well. And Leslie, for all the introvert and pink in the world is also not a bar person.

At this point, I'm not clear if I'm supposed to be the friend that says "I don't think this is a good idea" or the one who says, "Hell yeah!"

I always thought I was the former.

She did a little research and found out the tons of opportunities in Charlotte, North Carolina to do karaoke. I suggested her birthday be the target date.

Long story in a sentence: She totally chickened out and postponed karaoke but chose music bingo at a bar she'd been at twice with another friend.

Before we go in, we're talking about how she's supposed to move forward with so many unknowns and even more moving pieces.

"I've been realizing, Leslie, that the life we most want isn't going to come about the same way the life we had. I think for this one, we're supposed to just keep showing up. Just keep making the coffee and keep wanting what we most want."

Then we went in the bar.

Think Cheers vs. Coyote Ugly

With 40 rotating beers on tap.

And committed bartenders who WILL NOT give up until you find a beer you love. (#stoutgirl)

Add Bingo cards with songs from Motown, commercials, and one hit wonders, and you're pretty sure you'll dominate if sober.

We laughed and sang and toasted to our lives.

After two hours, all the prizes given (none of which we won), we had a few beers in us, and the night was over. Leslie goes to the bathroom.

A not-so-sober woman at the bar had a problem with the DJ's presentation of Bingo. She asked him to make it up to everyone.

He says into the microphone, "How about karaoke?"

She agrees, people cheer.

Sometime in the middle of her song, Leslie came out of the bathroom trying to not look at me- because we both know.

We just walked right into karaoke.

Long story in a sentence: Oh yes she did and to Queen's song "Somebody to Love" unrehearsed and knocked it out of the park. Wearing pink.

I'm more and more convinced that the life we most want, wants us too.

That when our soul calls, it doesn't do it in halves or pieces. Not in maybes or do-you-thinks.

Not in logic, or motivation, or pushing.

It requires something deeper than any of that because it's going to not face fear but run like water around it.

If we're lucky, there will be enough signs to satisfy our logical minds to we can give ourselves the gift of jumping in, cannonball, off the edge.

CHAPTER #202

Life Is Our Art

This past summer when Jordan said he was going back to LA, I ran away to a rare "open art studio" hosted by a local artist. His art is in galleries, retail stores (and I imagine) west coast beach homes, and NYC penthouses.

He randomly opens his studio to the public with the energy of Thelma and Louise driving over the cliff of creativity while offering to ride shotgun.

I snagged Leslie and Kait and we showed up to our own table, blank canvases and a warm welcome from the artist-who-shall-remain-nameless.

Instructions were something like, "The hardest part of all this is to start. Just put paint on the canvas. And keep doing that. My favorite part, and it always happens, is somewhere in the middle when you're not done but you have no clue what to do next. Go get water, take a walk, let it dry and come back to it. Other than that, have fun!" he walked away.

I came for Thelma and Louise and the only thing I hear now is Yoda. Every time he came over, truth began to overlay art.

I wasn't there to paint. I was there to splatter. I didn't want to think. I wanted to escape and create something that looked like life. White on white, a bit of blue and green, touches of yellow. I finished in like 15 min.

The artist came over, "Did you look at it from a distance?"

No.

He walked 10 feet away and magically, it appeared to not be done.

I worked some more, stepped back the obligatory 10 feet, and called him back over. Something was missing, although the splatters were everything I hoped for and then some.

He took his finger in coral peach paint and put a thumbprint on it.

"If you want someone to look at expensive earrings, what do you do?"

"Wear my hair up."

"Right. Because you're creating a focus. What do you see on your painting now?"

"The orange dot."

"Because there's a focus."

Wipes off the coral spot while telling me the theory of focus points, (however, whatever, wherever I want) but that every piece has one.

Did you ever just want someone to do it for you? Because you know they know what they're doing and you know you're making a mess? And you realize this is the middle that you were warned about and are supposed to have fun. And go walk and get water.

And air.

And did you ever realize that no one is coming to save you because you just stepped into some life lesson when all you came to do was splatter?

I have.

I figure out the f'ing focus. More splatters, heavy on the blue, bottom right. Ooh. More white. And a few dots on the bottom.

Stepping back 10 feet- I know I'm not done.

I find the artist, with a request, "I need texture."

He walks me back to The Closet of Surprises to his secret stash of supplies- brushes, paints, plastic instruments, knives, paper, and a swirl of items like guache that only artists understand. I choose a plastic comb, return to the table and happily RAKE across the canvas.

Because I am committed to wrecking it all like Thelma and Louise with Yoda buckled in the back seat.

Read: Super Duper No F'ing Clue.

But I'm starting to like it.

Stepping 10 feet back, I find the focus, like the colors, but it needs a little... something.

I go back to the artist-who-shall-remain-anonymous, "I have a focus. I'm done splattering. But it needs dimension. It needs a pop. I don't have a pop."

He returns to the Closet of Surprises and emerges with a box of paints.

Hands me the gold.

"Try this. Now, use it sparingly. Focus points."

He's trusting me with gold paint.

Because clearly, I came here to splatter, rake, and figure out how to create focus points — with gold.

Game. On.

So I did.

Splatter gold, rake, step back. *Voila.*

"Will you look over it? I think I'm done."

"If you're done, you're done. You don't need me to check it."

Because *why would this end any other way.*

Realizing it's not what I want to hear, he comes over and says, "It's not my painting, I don't know when it's done. "

I stand back and say, "It's done. I love it."

"Then it's done," and he walks back into his art closet never to be seen again. Kidding. He graciously ends the night with a group selfie.

It's the times I'm trying to Thelma and Louise my life in splattery, raking ways— partly flinging myself off a perceived cliff – that I find it. Partly being pushed to my edges, and partly committing to show up beyond all rational fear is always where the truth shows up.

Start.

The middle is coming — look forward to it but it's going to be tough.

Step back and look at it from a distance.

Don't give up in the middle.

Take a break. Come back.

Have fun.

Create a focus.

Step back and look at it from a distance.

Add layers.

Sprinkle with gold.

Say when you're done.

The experts don't say when you're done. Only you do.

It's your art.

#LifeIsOurArtandWeGetToSay

CHAPTER #203

48 Things Before 49

It's not like I know them and I'm done learning. It's like I know them and keep learning them. Again. Maybe just pick your favorite lottery numbers and read those- it's unapologetically a long list.

1. It will never be "sherbet." It's "sherbert."

2. Generic Q-Tips are never ever worth the money.

3. The person who says what and who I am is me.

4. I just don't like beer.

5. There is no extra time to play small.

6. Naps are non-negotiable.

7. I am and always will be a mom.

8. I can pretty much give up gluten, grain and sugar, if there are potato chips around.

9. I owe myself a black or brown leather jacket.

10. I will never ever be fearless. Removed from bucket list.

11. Truth is always worth waiting for. It *always* shows up.

12. People are not who I wish they were. Love anyway.

13.I am not to "earn" things — early bedtimes, carbs, long walks, or a kiss.

14. Red lipstick and I are BFF's. It's my fault I don't use it. But it's there when I'm ready.

15. I am not who people wish I was. It's ok.

16. I owe myself a stone washed denim jacket

17. I do not and never will like kale. Ever.

18. I'm a ninja at accepting who others are. It's worse to hope they

change.

19. I am done with the large slate and wood dinner table and 4 chairs. It's up for grabs. *Update: Not available- given to Habitat for Humanity.*

20. Never ever, ever make marshmallows from scratch again.

21. If something exhausts me, the only question I'm to ever ask is, "What am I carrying that's not mine? And for whom?"

22. Hellman's mayonnaise is the only one that counts.

23. Home is wherever I am.

24. I was once called in marriage counseling a "thoroughbred horse that needs to run in the fields and be tamed." I'm good with that now minus the tamed part.

25. I absolutely have no preference on potato chips except all of them.

26. The things that are too close to home and make me cry are half-baked and not for public consumption.

27. Just fearing less has and will always save my life.

28. Milky way over Snickers. But only twice a month — make it count.

29. Loss and grief are antidotes to perfection. And the back -door VIP pass to joy.

30. Martyring myself "to serve others" is ego driven spirituality. Stop immediately.

31. Whoever puts pickle juice in their deviled eggs can be my friend.

32. Apologies are my only lifeline back to others. They never have to take me back. I can apologize and not go back.

33. I will never ever have another dog until there's a man around who will take it to the vet to be put down. Ever.

34. Maya Stein's poem, "You Will Know," restores my soul.

35. The person who needs to be right is the one who will never be right enough. There's always more to be right about. Don't be that person.

36. I am no good at giving up coffee.

37. The antidote to being right is to listen. Just listen.

38. Live without being offended. Tend my yard.

39. It's ok that I bite my nails. Just give in.

40. Men TOTALLY will pursue me. When they don't, they're not worth chasing.

41. I commit to not healing crooked — on the crabby days, look behind for the trails of beauty, serendipity, and forgiveness. Heal strong.

42. Let others go.

43. I have a thing for pens. This will never change. They need to be medium—fine, around .05—.07— bright blue, gel, writes like butter. No grip. Must retract.

44. It is non-negotiable to want what I want.

45. Never just give my opinion. Ever. Always ask permission first.

46. I may never have it all mapped out. Or I may. Either way, just do the next thing. Even when it's just making coffee.

47. Listen to my body. It never lies.

48. God is love.

CHAPTER #204

Kale It Quits

Nobody wants to love kale more than I do.

It has more protein than even steak. And more fiber than Metamucil swirling in a glass.

It has more B vitamins than a complex B Vitamin from cyber Monday on Amazon.

And nearly a lifetime supply of Vitamin K.

Bet you don't even know what Vitamin K is. But it's a thing, trust me. Look it up.

Every doctor I've ever gone to has given me the Kale speech. "Hey, what you really need to be eating is kale.... protein, fiber, vitamin K."

So I've *wanted* to love kale.

I've eaten it raw and lightly steamed to perfection. I've practiced— I can get it to glow a green you only see in Ireland.

I've spent hours removing the spines and hiding it in soups. Hours. Because spines. Ew.

I've blended it in smoothies so well even I forgot it was in there.

I've tried it in cold pressed juices so expensive I could have bought a cold presser— whatever that is.

I've gotten the "right" kale. The curlier the better. Organic.

I've sent kids of farmers from the local farmer's markets to college over buying the "right" kale.

I've wasted entire bags of kale learning to roast it to perfection — throwing away recipes for roasted kale and talking to women in lines and produce sections in stores learning how to cook great kale.

Half a bag of kale makes an entire cookie sheet of roasted kale. Cookies are best on cookie sheets unless you are trying to love kale.

You know what's great about seasoned roasted kale?

The seasoning. That's it. And FYI, foodies, it doesn't play well with butter. Just EVOO. From Greece.

But I eat it because of the miracle food that it is, that everyone is convinced I need.

If I had an app that tracked how much time I've spent trying to love kale it would say 234,234 hours.

But guess what?

I've taken a food sensitivity blood test.

The lab verifies what I wished on the brightest star was true all along: I'm allergic to kale.

Not sneezing and eyes itching like I do with cats.

Nope. Just invisible inflammation that takes you out and makes you feel "meh" even when you're eating the world's miracle food that will wipe out every deficiency on the planet, and bring peace on earth and abundance to everyone including the financial markets in every country.

But not to me.

Honestly, it doesn't bother me that I'm allergic to kale.

Nor that I've tried to love it. Or learned how to cook it. Or pretended to like it so Jordan would eat it.

What bothers me to the point of regret, is that I didn't say four little words that would have saved actual weeks of my life.

I. Don't. Like. It.

That's all.

I. Don't. Like. Kale.

See? World is still here. Kale is even still here. The earth hasn't swallowed me whole instead of eating kale. We're good.

I didn't think I could say it.

Because experts. And miracle food.

And rejecting kale when you SAY you're all about health is basically lying about your commitment to living to 90.

And spinach is such a far second.... and why would I ever settle for "second best" according to everyone else? Not me. Woman up and love kale. Power through. Right?

And it's all true.. the experts, the miracle, the never settling for second best.

But not for me.

Not only do I loathe, despise, and detest it, in my body, it has the opposite effect.

Go figure.

So now I'm like, WHAT ELSE is supposed to be good for me that I. Don't. Like.???

I will not bore you with all the OTHER foods I actually love that I'm allergic to. Because it's not about food.

It's about finding, hearing, honoring what I need and don't need.

What matters and what doesn't.

And what is The Thing that I'm trying to love so hard for so long that really isn't good for me, and actually, I don't like, or that the time is over— even though mastered?

My question to myself this week as I've made decisions or spent time is this: Is It Kale?

Is it "good for me", and I "should" but something in the pit of my stomach is like Oh. Heck. No.

Life is too short to chase kale.

Grateful you're still here. Hope we can still be friends. It's ok if you like kale. I'll give you mine.

FYI— The Secret to Roasting Kale: wash it. dry it with paper towels completely. Cut out the spines. I'm serious.

Toss with oil in a bowl. Add salt, garlic, seasonings of any kind that you love. Put in oven at 415-420. After 4 minutes, turn every single leaf over and roast another 4 minutes. It will need another 2-3 min of roasting but that's it. It burns at the 4-minute mark. Trust me.

CHAPTER #205

9 Bookmarks

"So how was the retreat in the Outer Banks?" The retreat where I was pretty sure I was going to have to pretend to be Goldilocks and just enjoy 10 beds because I got a free upgrade and no one would come?

That retreat? ;-)

For those that measure in numbers, I tripled my attendance. On our reviews, out of 54 possible 10's we got 49. The others were nines. One eight but one 12. I've grown in staff, expanding from just me to Nichole, a chef and Leslie, a hot tub concierge, who also doubles as my right hand. Approximately one half of the attendees said they would be returning and bringing friends. Several women have already messaged me to save them a room for next year. That's the business side.

Now can we measure in what really matters?

I measure in moments, and tears, and smiles after sleeping in, uninterrupted, past 8:30am, and not being late.

I measure in shifts that alter faces, while scribbling notes in a journal that has become magic. Or the look I get when I say, "Come back at 6pm for dinner" and they have time to walk on the beach, cry, pray, finish projects, explore the area or sleep. To my surprise, for the long breaks no one asked me what they should do, or where they should go. It was as if everyone already felt their direction.

I measure in restaurant quality food with everyone asking for the recipe without ever realizing that these recipes were broken and rebuilt with love.

I measure in watching women who worked so hard to show up for themselves find connection to others effortless and serendipitous; or the ways they

I measure in how I felt inside the house, where space and time are measured in micro workshops, projects, and continuous Spotify playlists. And for that, I was at 1000 out of 10.

I can't tell the stories that aren't mine to tell.

I didn't even allow photos except for personal use. That's going to kill my social media "proof" for next year, but what happens in the OBX, stays in the OBX.

While I knew a bit of what people faced going home, I was looking forward to an empty house to rest.

Until the morning.

It was still an empty house.

But within hours, Jordan called asking how it all was and, "Did you get my birthday gift yet?"

Apparently, in the mail, was my gift that I absolved him of, knowing he was just restarting life in LA.

Nine bookmarks of our life—four images on each, non-repeating.

Mostly from his camera. His view.

I have makeup on in only three. Some I don't even have much hair.

Other days I'll never forget.

Banjo was there again.

I forgot how much we laughed.

I'm trying to figure out why didn't I ever think I was beautiful.

I remember these were all taken in "the worst years of my life" and I forgot how much love there was to lean on.

How all the times I was sure I was "wasting money" on a trip, or a dinner was a layer of memories that are in my cells.

These are the memories and cells I take with me when I'm on the retreat- teaching, listening, believing in, and making fires at night.

Maybe it's because of the 36 photos that we can get 49-10's.

Maybe all the "worst years" and "wasting money" taught me what really matters. If everything we do during the weekend doesn't impact real life, and transform real connections when everyone goes home -what are we doing here?

Because even today, although the house is empty, I'm not alone, and it's been my memories on 9 bookmarks I can stand on with very few regrets, and even more gratitude.

And apparently, I can finally say I'm a retreat leader. And a writer. And an adventurer. And to be grateful for everything it took to land me right here.

Thank you for all the cheering on. Ten points if you don't say *We already knew you were.*

Epilogue

It may be true that the antidote to fear is love … for ourselves, others, for our own fears themselves. I suspect that fears want love so they may be acknowledged so they can stop yelling, and tell us what they came to say and then move along.

Fear morphs inside us.

Sometimes it's ten red stoplights blinking.

Other times it's a nine- year-old scared child.

Sometimes it's a parent's voice saying, "You better not".

This is why I'll never be fearless- there will always be a form of fear somewhere.

My best bet, I've found is to make peace with fear, show up, and do the next thing anyway. This keeps my choices and perspective as 100% mine. But control went out the door in 2013. And the whole time, somewhere between me and God, I've been saving my life. This is not in spite of fear, but alongside it, not allowing it to derail, control or have a final say.

In the wake of our fears, maybe what's left treading water is our truest self. The one we've been carrying around all along. The self we've ignored because we were earning or proving or demanding of ourselves what we could never earn – worth, love, grace— because it was already ours.

"The time will come
when, with elation
you will greet yourself arriving
at your own door, in your own mirror
and each will smile at the other's welcome,
and say, sit here. Eat.

You will love again the stranger who was your self.
Give wine. Give bread. Give back your heart
to itself, to the stranger who has loved you
all your life, who you ignored
for another, who knows you by heart.
Take down the love letters from the bookshelf,
the photographs, the desperate notes,
peel your own image from the mirror.
Sit. Feast on your life."

---Derek Walcott,

Collected Poems, 1948–1984 (1986), *Steven Gould Axelrod (ed.) (2012). The New Anthology of American Poetry: Vol. III: Postmodernisms 1950—Present. Rutgers University Press.*

What Has Surprised Me

Remember those 1000 pieces I was trying to put back together? There actually were no border pieces. There wasn't even a picture on the box. Fractured from a life I had put together, what I've come to learn is that each piece is a tiny hologram that is still in me. All the pieces are there— not one missing.

Each a tiny moment that lives on.

Jordan learning to crawl, dealing with OCD, beating me in chess for the first time, giving the graduation speech in front of 250 people, making me dinner in Los Angeles.

My husband and I in Hawaii taking a first ever surf lesson, laughing on Saturdays at Panera's over bagels with Jordan, the way we agreed on a budget, and houses, and risk.

The days I ran our company, invoicing and checking twice, texting my husband questions and figuring out when the deliveries would land.

My friends laughing with me, telling me their husband and boyfriend stories while listening to mine as well. Rocking on the back deck, grateful we just understand.

Banjo barking at 2am, chasing squirrels, and running through the snow again, always the strong hunter.

Gram is still at the Thanksgiving table at our home, talking about the craft fair tomorrow and how great the autumn apple cake is.

Even Uncle John is telling me the Frayed Knot joke one more time, with a cigar in his hand and brandy swirling in his glass. He's going to let me blow the candles out on our birthday cake first, like he always does.

My scraggly, tired hair, trying to not break, is still trying to send me 100 signals that it can't take anymore as I sear it with the flat iron on a rainy day.

Grammy in her southern accent in her home at Candlewood Lake offering me chess pie while Daddy Joe is watching football. Sisters, aunts, uncles, cousins and cats opening gifts, playing board games, eating a ham sandwich and laughing. Always laughing.

It's all still in me.

Maybe you can't see it, but it all lives on…helping, reminding, teaching, hugging.

But there's a beautiful life that's emerging now because of all that, not in place of it. It's not a quick fix, but a slow unfolding.

Finding new recipes like a pumpkin and black bean chili that is made on Saturdays for the week ahead, simmering slowly while I go on an autumn walk.

The Mom Whisperer now rebranded with a keen eye and voice on what really does matter, how we really are enough. Videos uploaded and living on YouTube, freely offered, hoping to let a mom know she is never alone.

Lunch with a different friend each week. The ones whose hearts have been broken while not expecting mine to be completely healed.

A retreat for women who want to remember who they are.

Following intuition and signs and breadcrumbs even when they show up on a license plate saying "FINISHED" before a date even begins.

Writing, blogging, dating, laughing.

What's also surprised me is how quickly life falls apart and how slowly it takes to put it back together. But that it really does unfold, especially when I don't force or control every last movement.

What we all face is fear.

How we face it, is unique, sacred, and a process that we each have to take our time to work with in our own hearts. Thank you for coming along on my journey.

For being here.

For believing fear doesn't have to stop us.

For choosing to fear less in showing up to life — whether you're looking for the border pieces or taking a bucket list trip or starting to date.

For whatever your spiritual background or belief is, for knowing that love matters, and we're never alone.

For the holographic pieces of your life that are still in you and the way you carry them into your world, thank you. Because facing fear is always where we start. But where we end up is often more beautiful than we ever imagined. Truly, may we all find a life where everything we've ever wanted is on the other side of fearing just a little bit less.

Hi!

Would you help others find their way to this book? Please leave an honest review on Amazon!

It just may help others to feel less afraid and alone.

Thank you!

—

Vikki

Made in the USA
Coppell, TX
19 May 2026

77899652R00213